LOCOMOTION PAPERS

NORTHERN NORTHUMBERLAND'S MINOR RAILWAYS:

Volume Four

Limestone Industry Lines

by

Roger Jermy

THE OAKWOOD PRESS

© Oakwood Press & Roger Jermy 2012

British Library Cataloguing in Publication Data
A Record for this book is available from the British Library
ISBN 978 0 85361 706 8

Typeset by Oakwood Graphics.
Repro by PKmediaworks, Cranborne, Dorset.
Printed by Information Press Ltd, Eynsham, Oxford.

All rights reserved. No part of this book may be reproduced or transmitted in any form or by any means, electronic or mechanical, including photocopying, recording or by any information storage and retrieval system, without permission from the Publisher in writing.

This book is dedicated to my first granddaughter, Poppy

From the same author

Northern Northumberland's Minor Railways:
Volume One: Brickworks, Forestry, Contractors, Military Target railways and various other lines (ISBN 978 0 85361 703 7)

Northern Northumberland's Minor Railways:
Volume Two: Colliery & Associated Lines
(ISBN 978 0 85361 704 4)

Northern Northumberland's Minor Railways:
Volume Three: Sandstone, Whinstone & Gravel Lines
(ISBN 978 0 85361 705 1)

Front cover: HE268/181 is the only steam locomotive which worked at Little Mill limeworks that has been positively identified. Arriving in 1907, it moved wagons of lime and coal on the 2 ft 6 in. gauge system until around the time of World War II, when it was replaced by a 'home-made' engine. After the war's end it remained, as here, on a short length of track until it was scrapped around February 1951. *J.W. Armstrong Trust*

Published by The Oakwood Press (Usk), P.O. Box 13, Usk, Mon., NP15 1YS.
E-mail: sales@oakwoodpress.co.uk
Website: www.oakwoodpress.co.uk

Contents

Introduction

For the purpose of this book 'Northern Northumberland' is regarded as encompassing that area of the county lying within the administrative district of Berwick-upon-Tweed and Alnwick. Until the mid-19th century part of the area covered lay within the County of Durham.

The term 'Minor Railways' is used in this book to include lines variously referred to as railways, tramways, wag(g)onways and craneways, whether of narrow or standard gauge, which were not owned or operated by the 'main line' railway companies. Thus lines, such as the Rothbury branch, or Alnwick to Coldstream branch, do not feature as they were part of the North British Railway (NBR) and North Eastern Railway (NER) respectively. Later both became part of the London & North Eastern Railway (LNER) and British Railways (BR). Similarly this book does not cover lines which were essentially worked as sidings from main lines, such as those servicing Easington Quarry at Belford, or the dockside branch railway at Tweedmouth.

No attempt has been made to convert former imperial units into their present day metric equivalents. Units appropriate to the time of each railway have been used. Thus boiler pressures, for example, are referred to in pounds per square inch and costs are described in pounds, shillings and pence where the original source materials used these. Where metric units have appeared in original documents they have been retained.

The lines covered in this series of books were constructed for a wide variety of purposes. Some were associated with the many quarries, whether limestone, whinstone or sandstone, in the area. Others were linked with the coal mining industry. Some served brick and tile works, whilst others were built for military purposes. The forestry and timber industries were responsible for the creation of some lines and in recent years small lines have been constructed for the tourist industry. Almost exactly 200 years of local railway history are covered in these books. This, the last book in the series, concentrates on the limestone industry.

Whilst it has been necessary to include some technical railway details it has also been considered important to place the railways into their social, geographical and historical context. Hopefully this will widen the readership of the book. The purist may consider it an important omission that lists of source materials and references have not been included after each chapter. If readers wish to make an individual study of the sources that have been consulted then they are cordially invited to get in touch with me via the publisher.

Whilst researching for the book it has been considered a top priority that original sources be consulted, and that visits be made to as many of the sites as is practicable or possible. Oral ('anecdotal') evidence, and evidence from secondary sources, such as newspaper reports, has been used on various occasions. However, memories, particularly of events that happened nearly a century ago, may have become clouded, and every effort has been made to find written material which corroborates the evidence of the spoken word. On occasions it has been realized that the details reproduced here differ from previously published material. Hopefully I am correcting earlier errors rather than introducing new ones. Nevertheless I accept full responsibility for any mistakes in the text.

At many points in the book I have referred to lines or their remains being on private property. Permission must *always* be sought from landowners or tenants

Beadnell limekilns with fishing boats in the foreground. *Author's Collection*

before visits are attempted. In certain cases the sites of railways, or former railways, can pose considerable danger to visitors, for example from steep cliffs or quarry faces, falling rocks, marshy ground or deep water. The surviving military railways pose a particular threat as they are located within still-active training areas where live ammunition is used. Visits to these lines are extremely dangerous if not carefully supervised by appropriate expert personnel. The flying of red flags, the display of red lights and the presence of secure fences indicate danger and the instructions on warning notices should be followed.

This book, whilst attempting to be comprehensive, cannot claim to have included every detail about these railways. Written records of some railways are sparse or incomplete, and, in the case of many of the lines, there is no one still alive with personal memories to impart. The author would therefore welcome the receipt of any information, perhaps from family histories or albums, which adds to the story of any of the lines. Old photographs or postcards, for which the author has been searching for several years, can provide valuable insight into the working of a line. However, in researching this final book in the series the author has been handicapped by the very early demise of some of the limeworks and their railways. Those at Beadnell, Seahouses and Ancroft, for example, had closed before the mid-point of the 19th century, well before cameras became common. Just two limeworks survived in the area until after the end of World War II. As a result photographs showing the quarries or kilns 'in action' have been very difficult to obtain. It is fortunate, in the case of Holy Island, that a 19th century artist painted such accurate paintings of the lime jetty. Fortunately the author has been able to access most of the sites to record some of the industrial archaeological remains. However, it would be a pleasure to receive details of any other photographs or paintings that exist of these sites.

In various places in the text, locomotive builders names have been abbreviated; a key to these abbreviations appears on page 134.

Roger Jermy
Alnwick, Northumberland
2012

Chapter One

The Limestone Industry in Northern Northumberland

The pattern of the solid geology of northern Northumberland was detailed in Volume Three of this series. The limestone rocks date from the Carboniferous period (some 350-275 million years ago) and are contained within the cementstone layers which form a crescent shape, extending from the hinterland of Berwick in the north down to the border with the Castle Morpeth District. The bands of limestone are found in association with soft shales (containing iron nodules), coal measures and some sandstone. The limestone was laid down in shallow, warm seas. In places it is quite hard and fossil-free, but the softer limestones often contain fossils such as small corals, molluscs and crinoid stems. Where it is softer, almost crumbly in texture, it may be coloured brownish due to the presence of iron. In some places, such as the north coast of Holy Island, the limestone layers are exposed and form part of the sea cliffs. Elsewhere some limestone can be quarried only after removal of overburden. Various limestone bands have been quarried commercially including the so-called Acre and Eelwell Limestones.

Limestone quarrying has been of importance for thousands of years, having its origins in the early Middle Eastern civilizations, and in the Greek and Roman empires. As well as being used in the building industry, lime has been used during the preparation of hides (in leather making), in the chemical industry, at iron- and gasworks and in agriculture for 'sweetening', or neutralizing, acid soils. It is also used for breaking up the soil in areas where clay is heavy or in gardens where lime-loving crops, such as brassicas, are grown. In Northern Northumberland there are many, mainly inland, areas where the soil is peaty and acidic and where it has been necessary to add lime to improve the soil for crops. Much lime has been used locally in the manufacture of lime mortar, for bridges, viaducts and buildings. Some has been used as a wash for the outside of buildings. Whilst much of the locally quarried lime has been used within Northern Northumberland, some has been 'exported' by sea, for example from the ports of Seahouses, Beadnell, Tweedmouth and Holy Island, to Scotland and even the near-continent. The coming of the main line railways facilitated the transport of some lime to the developing industrial areas of Tyneside.

Limestone is largely composed of calcium carbonate. When heated in a kiln at over 1,000º celsius it breaks down, releasing carbon dioxide, and becoming quicklime (calcium oxide). Approximately two tons of limestone produce one ton of quicklime. Quicklime is a difficult and dangerous chemical to handle and transport as it reacts violently when water is added, liberating much heat. If this is done in controlled conditions, such as on the 'slaking floor' of a limeworks, the quick lime can be converted, by the gradual addition of water, to slaked lime. It is slaked lime that is generally transported from a limeworks. Though slaked lime is alkaline, it is less harmful than quicklime, and can be added directly to acid soils for their neutralization. If used to make lime mortars it absorbs carbon dioxide from the air and is reconverted into the hard calcium carbonate. A similar process occurs if a lime wash is applied to the walls of buildings.

Lime kilns in northern Northumberland have a variety of shapes and sizes, but all were built with a lining of firebricks to resist the high temperatures used in the process of roasting the limestone ('calcining'). Normally about a ton of coal was required to roast four to five tons of limestone. Sometimes a kiln would consist of a single 'pot' and the limestone was roasted in batches. However, larger kilns could contain up to six pots thus increasing efficiency and output.

In the northern Northumberland area rail lines, usually of narrow gauge, first became associated with limestone quarries and limeworks at the end of the 18th century. Their use continued for about 150 years, until the middle of the 20th century. Fortunately many kilns survive, some actively preserved, and the surviving embankments and cuttings indicate the former routes of the associated rail lines. Many such lines are identified as 'Old tramway' or 'Old wagonway' on Ordnance Survey maps, and aerial photographs often confirm the position and extent of these former lines.

The rail lines could perform several vital functions. Firstly limestone could be transported from the quarry faces to charge the kilns. Secondly the fuel, usually coal, could be brought to the kiln top in the same way. Finally a rail line would facilitate removal of the roasted lime from the kilns to the slaking floor. Occasionally the proximity of a harbour or jetty would permit the unloading of the lime wagons directly into the holds of vessels. This occurred at Holy Island, for example. Elsewhere loading banks allowed transfer of lime into standard

Northern Northumberland possesses many limekilns, some of which have been restored, whereas others are in need of some repair and restoration. This prominent kiln, situated at Harlow Hill, near Longhoughton and photographed from the Littlehoughton road, is in fair condition. No tramway associated with this kiln has yet been identified. *Author*

gauge rail wagons, such as those at Little Mill or Scremerston. In later years the contents of the wagons could be transferred to road vehicles for distribution, such as at the Greenleighton works. In early years the rail wagons were wooden-sided, though later, metal-sided side-tipper wagons were commonly employed.

Over short distances man-power could be used to propel smaller wagons of limestone or coal. The larger works and those with longer rail lines, often employed horse-power. In the late 19th and then the 20th centuries a few concerns operated either steam or diesel locomotives. Almost invariably, the rail lines associated with the northern Northumberland limeworks were of narrow gauge, though standard gauge sidings were often present where the works were located adjacent to main lines, Little Mill, Scremerston and Ritton White House being examples. One limestone railway system, namely that at Greenleighton, employed a standard gauge line for some years, though after an initial closure and a subsequent reopening, it became served by a narrow gauge line.

Some of the limeworks described in this volume were of limited size, had only a handful of employees, and their railways were very short. Others, such as the Sandbanks works at Scremerston or that on Holy Island, had more extensive systems and upwards of 40 workmen were employed. Some of these laboured in the quarries, some serviced the kilns and slaking floors, whilst others operated the small railways or repaired the equipment. A limeworks could be a dangerous place and there are records relating to the deaths in the area of both workmen and horses at the kiln top, either by suffocation or by accidentally falling into the kilns. Lime has corrosive properties and medical records show that eye and lung damage was common amongst employees exposed to the dust.

Although there are whinstone and sandstone quarries in the area still producing huge quantities of stone well into the 21st century, all of the lime works have long-since closed, the last being W.T. Bathgate's kiln at Greenleighton which was fired for the last time in the late 1960s. Some limestone was, however, quarried at Greenleighton as recently as 1982 in connection with the building of the Kielder dam and reservoir. This was probably the last time that limestone would be used on a commercial scale in the northern Northumberland area.

Most of the limeworks and railways described in this book had closed before the start of the 20th century and others closed in that century's early years. Consequently it has proved very difficult to find 'action' pictures of the works and their rail lines. Fortunately a few photographers thought it was worthwhile to point their cameras in the direction of the works, their wagons or their locomotives. In the case of the Holy Island which closed in the 1880s we are even more fortunate in that an artist, with an eye for accurate detail, chose to record the loading and unloading of horse-drawn tubs on that island's rail system. For many of the limeworks and their railways we must be content with the present-day remains of the kilns and associated earthworks to remind us of the railways, tramways and wagonways of this formerly important industry in the north of Northumberland.

Chapter Two

The Limestone Tramways of the Berwick Coast

Several early limekilns, producing lime for local agricultural or domestic purposes, were located on the coast near Scremerston, south of Berwick. The later, larger, limeworks which developed on the same coast were primarily built for the purpose of producing lime for distribution via links to the main East Coast main line, though some lime was used locally. This railway line, opened in the late 1840s, runs near to the coast for much of its route through the north of the county. The Saltpan How works lacked sidings from the main line and therefore used horse-drawn carts to take its lime to a loading bank near to Scremerston station, where transhipment occurred into standard gauge wagons. The larger Seaside or Sandbanks works had, at different times, two different rail connections to the main line, facilitating the arrival of coal fuel and the removal of loaded wagons of lime. It is recorded that some of the lime was exported from the port of Tweedmouth.

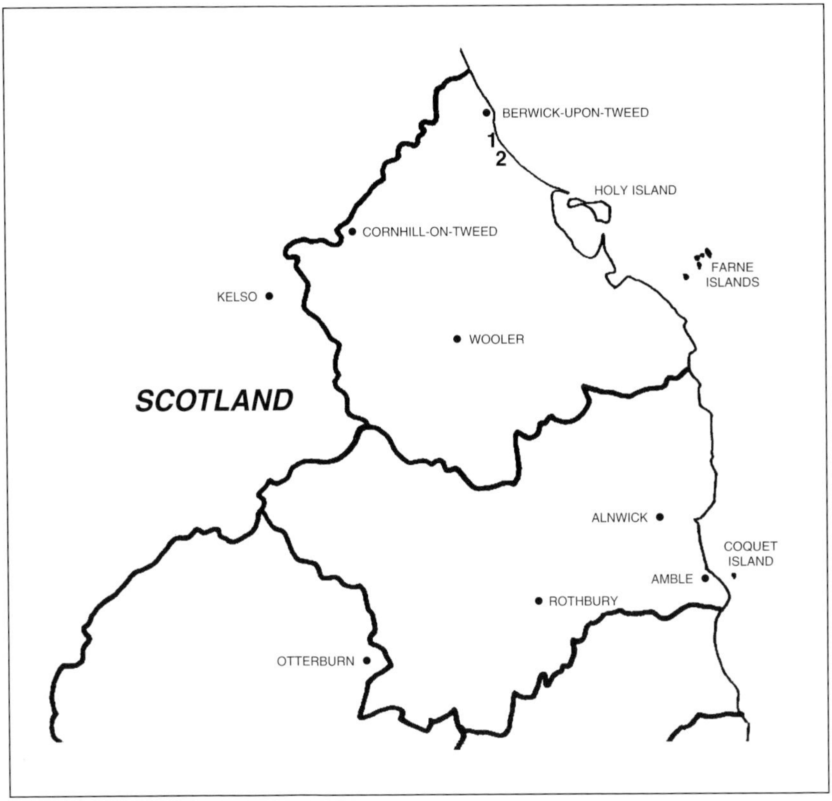

This is one of the very old kilns on the Berwick coast which preceded the limeworks at Saltpan How and Scremerston Sandbanks. Its lime was drawn from the quarry which would later supply the Sandbanks Works. Its lime output was largely for agricultural purposes and its proximity to the coast would have allowed some movement by coastal vessels. *Author*

This is a 2011 view of the now-closed Scremerston station on the East Coast main line. Beyond the station the road passes the site of Saltpan How works and terminates at the site of Scremerston Sandbanks limeworks. The station is now a private house. *Author*

1 - The Saltpan How Limeworks Railway at Scremerston

Saltpan How (sometimes written as 'Howe') was the first, but smaller, of the two 19th century limeworks that were situated near the coast at Scremerston (in Ancroft parish) to the south east of Berwick-upon-Tweed and Tweedmouth. It was located 100 yards inland from the south end of Saltpan Rocks (NU024489). Nicholas Weatherley's survey of the area for the Greenwich Hospital estates resulted in a map being published in 1824 which is entitled 'Scremerston Colliery and Lime Works'. It shows Saltpan How kiln (identified as 'Kiln Banks') and a further kiln, named South Saltpan How, a short distance away. A small quarry was sited nearby. Other documented evidence of a limeworks on this site appears in the Parson & White Local Directory of 1828 in which Robert Carr is described as 'Farmer and Limeburner at Saltpan How'. The sale of some other small local lime kilns at Scremerston appeared in the *Berwick Advertiser* of 3rd May, 1823.

The works are clearly shown on the first edition Ordnance Survey map of the 1860s, reproduced below, which indicates a quarry facing inland from the sea. The map shows two 'sidings' serving the quarry faces, leading to a wagon turntable within the quarry. From the turntable, the line, with the aid of a sharp curve or reversal, leads to a single pot kiln which was located to the west of the quarry. It is likely that man power or, perhaps, horsepower was used to move the wagons of lime (*see below*). The coal for roasting the lime would likely have been delivered by cart from one of the nearby Scremerston pits.

Unlike the larger Scremerston (or Seaside) Limeworks at Sandbanks further down the coast, the Saltpan How works was not linked via a siding to the adjacent Newcastle to Berwick main line and its lime was removed from the site by horse-drawn cart to a lime depot located at Scremerston station. This lay a

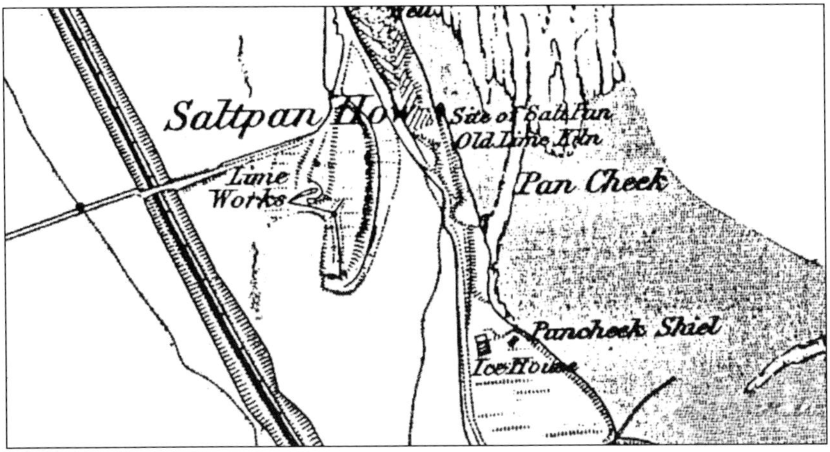

Saltpan How limeworks was located between the main line railway and the low cliffs at Scremerston, close to an earlier kiln and a 'pan' where salt was extracted from seawater. The Saltpan How lime was transported by cart either for local use or for onward movement by main line train. *Ordnance Survey, Crown Copyright, All Rights Reserved*

The lime siding at Scremerston was under the supervision of the station master at Scremerston station. The siding was located, beyond the level crossing, on the east side of the main line adjacent to the 'up track'. Today only the width of the railway property at this point suggests the former existence of the siding. *Author*

This is the site of the lime siding, adjacent to the Scremerston level crossing, to which the lime from Saltpan How was carted. The gate allows access to Network Rail staff visiting and inspecting the various buildings on the site. *Author*

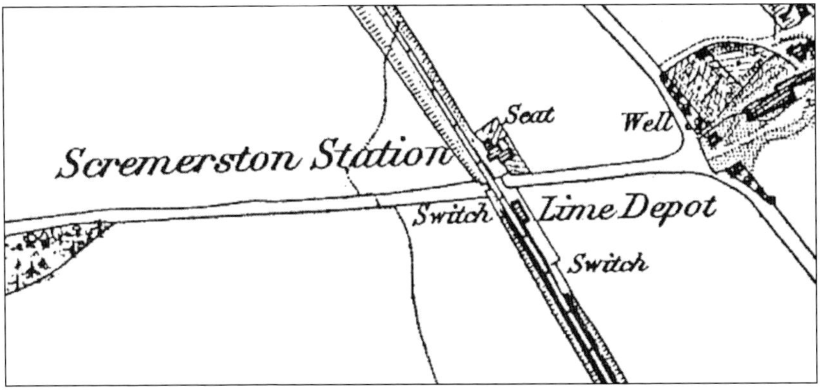

This early Ordnance Survey map shows Scremerston lime depot which was located on the opposite side of the level crossing from Scremerston station. Lime was carted to here from Saltpan How lime works. *Ordnance Survey, Crown Copyright, All Rights Reserved*

short distance to the north of the works along the coastal track. The lime depot was located on the east side of the main line immediately to the south of the level crossing. From here the lime was taken away by the North Eastern Railway.

By the date of the second edition Ordnance Survey maps the lime works had been closed, the quarry being unmarked and the railway removed. The kiln itself was to be identified on maps until the 1950s when the whole of the quarry site was filled in with tons of Berwick's domestic rubbish. A survey of 1976 revealed very little in terms of industrial remains. Today a casual visitor would be unaware of the former existence of a quarry, wagonway and limeworks at the site! The nearby station at Scremerston closed to passengers on 8th July, 1951 though some of its buildings survive in private ownership. The lime siding is long-since removed though its former site can be seen on the south side of the level crossing.

The workmen at the quarry and limeworks lived in the Saltpan How Cottages (described as a 'village' on the census return despite there being only seven cottages), though after this works closed some were occupied by the families of men employed at the Seaside works at Sandbanks to the south. These cottages were located to the east side of the coastal track to the north of the quarry. In 1851 a total of eight 'limestone miners' lived in these cottages with a further two living at the hamlet of Philadelphia close by, and two at Hillhead Farm. A lad was employed as a 'Waggon [*sic*] Driver at the Quarry', perhaps indicating the use of a horse to move the wagons. By 1861 there were still seven quarrymen living at Saltpan How cottages. By this year, however, the Sandbanks or Seaside works was in full operation and the foreman and 19 men lived in the cottages which had been specially built for this workforce. It is likely that some of the 15 men living at Philadelphia also found employment at the new works. However, by 1881 some of the cottages were uninhabited following the closure of the Saltpan How quarry, works and railway.

Parts of the stone faces at the Scremerston Sandbanks quarry are still exposed despite erosion caused by the weather and grazing animals. The routes of several of the quarry tramways can still be followed, some being used as footpaths. *Author*

The huge embankment is the remains of the incline up which the tubs of lime were hauled from the Sandbanks Quarry towards the kiln top. This view is taken from a point adjacent to a World War II gun emplacement which was located near to the kiln loading point. No traces of the rails remain. *Author*

2 - *The Scremerston (Seaside or Sandbanks) Limeworks Railways*

> I was born 80 years ago at a place called Philadelphia, one of the houses midway between Salt Pan How and Sandbanks. I well remember the limeworks where my father was employed and seeing the little trucks hauled to the top of the kiln by an engine on top of the kiln, having been brought part of the way by a horse from the quarry west of the main line opposite Philadelphia.

These words were written by Tom Brown and recorded in the *Berwick Bulletin* of 8th October, 1980, though written somewhat earlier. He was one of the last, if not the last person, to remember the working Sandbanks Limeworks (sometimes referred to as 'Seaside Limeworks') at Cocklawburn, Scremerston (NU 031481). This was the larger of the two local limeworks and was located to the south of the Saltpan How works. Though most of the Sandbanks output of lime was taken away by rail, a small amount was sold for use on local farms. This latter was collected from the works by horse-drawn carts.

Like the Saltpan How limeworks, the Scremerston Sandbanks limeworks lay on the land of the Greenwich Hospital, formerly owned by the Earl of Derwentwater. Drawn in 1824, the Greenwich Hospital map shows that Saltpan How works was the major limeworks on the coast at Scremerston at that time. At the future site of the larger Sandbanks works there was just a small quarry and an old lime kiln (*see accompanying photograph*). The growth of the limeworks at Sandbanks was linked to the demise of the Saltpan How works around the 1850s-1860s.

The first edition Ordnance Survey map, dating from the 1860s, shows the quarry and works site at Sandbanks in much detail. There were quarries to both the south and the north of the works, each served by lines of narrow gauge tramway. In addition there was a connection to the North Eastern Railway's main Newcastle to Berwick line. The absence of a similar connection to the Saltpan How works probably contributed to its demise.

The quarries to the south of the works were located close to the cliff top, some 50 feet above sea level but they stretched inland for over 100 yards. The earliest workings had been towards the inland side of the quarry, the later workings were closer to the cliff top. The tramway, in the 1860s, was serving these later workings. It left the quarry face heading south-west but at the quarry entrance performed a 90º turn to the right as it approached the base of the incline leading to the kiln top. Here, just beyond the smithy building, the horse would be uncoupled from the wagons and the cable, powered by the engine and winch near the kiln top, would take over haulage. The winch hauled the wagons up through the cutting and then the embankment with their steep gradient. The detail on the map is not very clear at the kiln top but it appears to show a small wagon turntable and a couple of short wagon sidings. This length of tramway was known to the workers as the 'Southside'.

The quarries to the north and north-west of the works were located a short distance inland. The earliest workings were to the north, away from the main railway line but gradually the quarry faces were moved westwards until the quarry was very close to the railway. Some quarrying took place to the west of the main line with a tunnel beneath this to allow the stone to be brought to the limeworks (*see Tom Brown's account*). However, this probably took place for only

This is the World War II gun emplacement at the top of the Sandbanks incline. The limekiln was located a few yards to the east of this point. *Author*

This level area is the site of the former Sandbanks limeworks. The kilns were in the centre of the picture with the siding-link to the main line leading to the right. Apart from the foundations of some of the former works cottages, the embankment and incline are the only remains of the works. *Author*

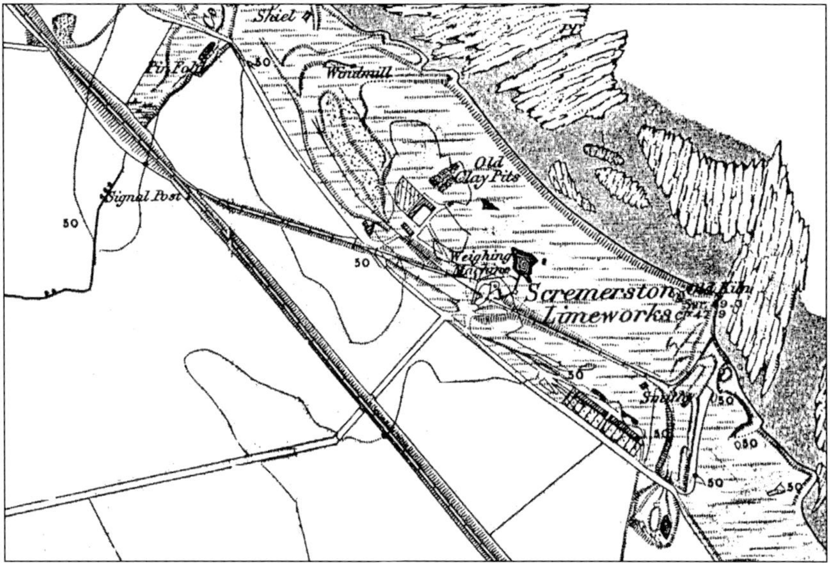

This map, surveyed in the 1860s, shows the tramways linking the quarries (to both north and south of the works) with the kilns of the Sandbanks Limeworks. The standard gauge branch from the main line is shown leading to the works sidings. The branch was moved slightly towards the south just a few years after this map was drawn with a signal box being constructed at the new junction. *Ordnance Survey, Crown Copyright, All Rights Reserved*

a short period and a site survey failed to reveal the location of the tunnel which was presumably filled in. The rail line for these quarries was known as the 'Northside' and its route to the top of the kilns crossed over the standard gauge sidings, perhaps by means of a trestle bridge, for there are no remains of an embankment to the kiln top from this direction. Once again the wagons were horse-drawn.

In the vicinity of the kiln were located the stables, a grinder for reducing the size of the lime to a fine powder, and a weighbridge for measuring the amount of lime taken out by each wagon onto the main line railway. The link with the main line consisted of a single line with a loop at the works end. There was an additional siding for standard gauge wagons to the south of the kiln.

A newspaper description of an accident which happened at this point (when an express hit an empty wagon which had strayed onto the main line) indicates the mode of working of the standard gauge sidings. A southbound train with wagons for the limeworks would arrive on the main line. It would reverse into the limeworks siding and the locomotive would uncouple from the empty wagons, with a 'stop block' being placed to prevent their movement. Once the empties had been left, the locomotive would head over the facing points towards the limeworks where it would collect the loaded wagons. It would then reverse and pull its load back into the sidings by the main line. A final reversal over the crossover onto the down line allowed the train of 'fulls' to head off for

A down East Coast train heads for Berwick-upon-Tweed and Edinburgh, passing the site of the former loop and sidings of the Scremerston Sandbanks limeworks. The 'kink' in the fence identified the exact point where the works line left the loop and headed for the works. A signal box was located on the far side of the main line opposite the junction. *Author*

In a photograph taken from the site of the former kiln top at Sandbanks, locomotive 71000 *Duke of Gloucester* speeds northwards towards Edinburgh with a rail tour in 2011. The former siding to the limeworks crossed the field in the foreground from the loop adjacent to the main line. *Author*

Tweedmouth. It is likely that the 'sidings' included a loop so as to allow a brake van to be attached correctly at the rear of the train. The empty wagons waited at the siding until they were collected by horses from the works. The Ordnance Survey maps fail to show the track layout in detail; however a signal post is marked next to the junction.

The siding was usually worked by 'the pilot engine' from Tweedmouth. Usually there was one trip per day to the works, occasionally more. Usually three wagons of coal were brought to the works daily plus the 'empties' for loading with lime, with about four wagons of lime being taken away.

By the early 1890s quarrying to the north-west of the limeworks had necessitated the moving of the connection with the main line to a point about 100 yards further to the south. The OS maps indicate that by this time a signal box had been erected opposite the junction to control movements to and from the limeworks. A long loop is shown to the side of the up line, with the line to the limeworks leaving from approximately halfway along its length. This 'new' line curved more sharply than the former one and approached the works on a very different alignment. There was still a loop at the end of the line, together with a small siding only approachable after reversal. The line approached the loading area under what has been described as a 'trellis work of metal girders'. A short siding, presumably to store wagons, was still located to the south of the kilns. The map indicates that there were three 'pots' at the kiln which explains some recorded observations that the works burned lime continuously: one kiln being loaded, one fired and one being emptied of lime.

By this time the 'Northside' tramway had already been lifted and all limestone was being brought to the kilns from the northern quarry by cart, though the 'Southside' line still carried stone originating in the quarry close to the top of the cliff above Far Skerr rocks. However quantities of stone carried on the 'Southside' were decreasing as quarrying became concentrated to the north of the works.

The main lessee of the works was John Evelyn Carr who was also a Director of the Scremerston Coal Co. (until his death in 1894). He lived at 'Seahouse' close to Scremerston station. His managers were Ralph Richardson (1850s), John Richardson (see 'Little Mill', *Chapter Six*) who was in turn succeeded by his son Alex, originally appointed to look after the works engine. (Alex Richardson subsequently left Scremerston to work at the limeworks at Little Mill.) The final Manager, at the time of closure, was a George Forsyth. Messrs Brown & Purvis later looked after the haulage engine whilst Charlie Blythe 'rode the trucks of stone'. Some 19 men were employed at the works under the Manager. A few were born locally (at, for example, Lowick, Barmoor, Beal, Chatton and Holy Island) but others originated from as far south as Jarrow or from Scotland to the north. Census records show that a few had transferred from closed limeworks elsewhere. Some lived in the 10 works cottages known as 'Sandbanks', whilst others lived at Philadelphia or Saltpan How to the north.

In the second half of the 1890s the pattern of obtaining the limestone changed. The bands of limestone dipped inland at an angle of about 1 in 60 and it was decided to mine, rather than quarry, the stone in order to save the time and costs associated with the removal of increasing amounts of clay overburden. The band of limestone was 24 inches in thickness at this point and by the time

The link from the main line to the limeworks passed through the site of this present-day gate. The HST is passing the site of the loop where the link met the main line. Looking in the opposite direction through the gate, reveals the sidings where standard gauge wagons, either empties awaiting loading, or 'fulls' were stabled. The incline, which led the narrow gauge tubs of stone to the kiln top is in the background. Some quarry cottages were formerly located to the far right of this view.
(Both) Author

of closure of the works a complex network of mine passages and chambers led some 30 yards underground. Substantial pillars of stone had to be left to prevent collapse. No tramway lines were constructed into the mines, all limestone being removed by horse-drawn cart to the kilns. How many of the three kilns were still being fired is not known but the quantities of stone being processed were much reduced. The original stables were still in use. The 'Abandoned Mine Plan' (dated January 1901) suggests that all tramway rails had been lifted by the time of closure. Furthermore the sidings linked to the main line had also been lifted and all of the rails had been sold, their former route being marked by a curving field boundary fence. The last of the lime was, presumably, all dispatched by road.

There is one recorded instance of a serious accident at Sandbanks. One of the men working in the quarry was run down by a wagon which was descending an incline, and he suffered serious injuries.

The works had actually closed in November 1900 and many of the men moved to work in the Scremerston Colliery. For a short time, concrete blocks, bricks, paving slabs and breeze blocks were made near to Sandbanks cottages, some of which were, by now, unoccupied. The cottages were eventually demolished prior to World War II and the demolition of the kilns, at a cost of £1,500, was reported in the *Berwick Advertiser* of 12th February, 1981. Some of the quarries, especially those to the north of the works were used to bury rubbish from Berwick-upon-Tweed and Tweedmouth. The land has been restored to somewhat undulating farmland.

Today it is possible to drive to the Sandbanks site from the A1 road by following the road which is signposted 'Cocklawburn Beach'. Initially this is a good metalled road, but after the level crossing and beach access it becomes a rough and pitted gravel track. However, there is parking for several vehicles at the end of the track, adjacent to the location of the former works. It is a straightforward walk along the footpath from the car parking area to the quarries to the south of the works, there to follow some of the tramway routes towards the quarry faces. Use of reproductions of the old OS maps allows identification of the site of the former works cottages though little remains of these apart from some walls and rubble. Return can be made via the cutting and embankment, at the upper end of which there is an unsightly concrete World War II gun emplacement. This commanded a view towards Holy Island and formed part of the coastal defences against invasion. The location of the former loop and siding is still identifiable below with the aid of old maps.

(An old kiln, which predates the Sandbanks works, survives close to the cliff top near the main quarry though it is isolated by a barbed wire safety fence. Great care should be taken when approaching this kiln! It is best viewed from the beach below. It obtained its limestone from the small area of quarry located to its west side.)

Although the public have unrestricted pedestrian access to most of the area around the Sandbanks Limeworks site, the now-indistinct alignments of the former rail links with the main line cross private farmland. The area is designated as a Site of Special Scientific Interest (SSSI) and, as such, there are certain restrictions on human activities such as camping or lighting fires.

Coves Quarry was used to supply limestone to the St Cuthbert's limeworks though, being right on the coast, it was not a reliable source as high tides and storms covered the lower part of the workings with water. Seaweed can be seen on the quarry floor in this picture postcard view.
Author's Collection

Nessend Quarry was sheltered behind the sea cliffs and was unaffected by tides or storms. The quarry faces are visible in this 1980s photograph and in certain parts of the quarry it is still possible to pick out the routes of the former rail lines between piles of quarried stone and spoil.
Author

Chapter Three

The Holy Island Limestone Waggonways

The Holy Island of Lindisfarne lies off the coast of Northumberland, though it can be reached by a road causeway at low tide. Beneath the boulder clay, left behind in the last Ice Age, and the windblown sand, lie rock layers of limestone, shale with ironstone nodules, sandstone and coal. Some of the ironstone was shipped to Falkirk in Scotland by the Carron Iron Company in the early 19th century and some coal was mined in the same century for local use. However, it was the presence of limestone that gave rise to what became the island's principal industry of the mid-1800s.

3 - The St Cuthbert's Limeworks Waggonway

(Most of the surviving documentation relating to the *early* rail lines on Holy Island uses the term 'waggonway' rather than wagonway or tramway. Accordingly this is the term that will first be used here, along with the term 'waggon' for the vehicles used to transport the lime and coal. In documents relating to the *later* lines the term 'tramway' is more commonly used.)

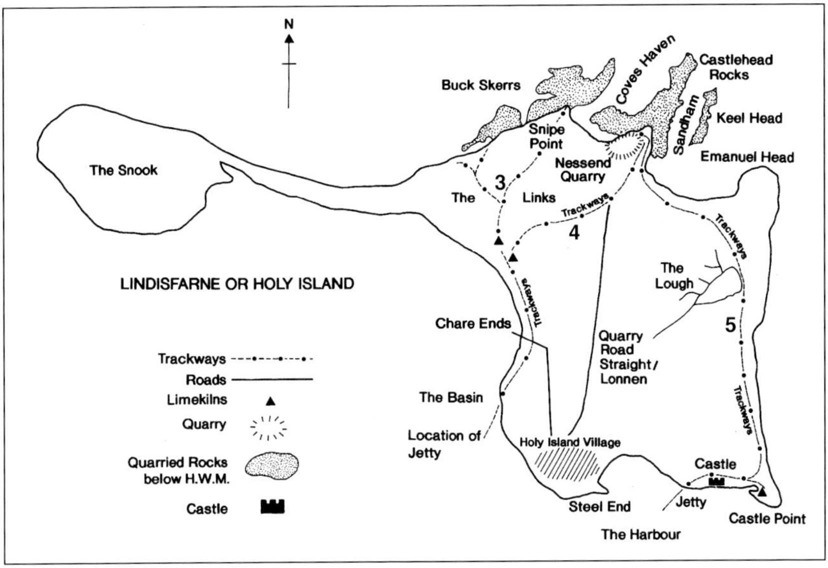

This composite map shows the various limestone waggonways that existed on the island at different periods. The first linked the north coast, including Coves Quarry, with St Cuthbert's limeworks on the Links. The second linked Nessend Quarry with the short-lived Kennedy limeworks, also on the Links, whilst the third linked the same quarry with the Castle Point limeworks.. *Author*

Mid-19th century quarrying activities in Nessend Quarry were unlikely to have been captured by photographers! However, the artist has produced this drawing of what it might have looked like. The drawing is based on photographs of early 'tubs' and pictures of quarrymen at other local quarries in the 19th century. Many of these quarrymen were Scots or Irish. *Peter Westley*

This second Peter Westley drawing shows the Kennedy limeworks. As explained in the text these kilns were in action for a very brief period before being replaced by the Castle Point kilns. Their site, and the long approach embankment for the waggonway, can still be readily identified in the early 21st century. Lindisfarne Castle is shown in the background; in the 1850s its outline differed from that of the present day. *Peter Westley*

There is some evidence for the quarrying for limestone on Holy Island in the late 18th century. However, this was on a small scale. It was not until 1839, when John Selby inherited the Lordship of the Manor, that the potential of the limestone deposits was to be realized. Selby applied to the Crown Commissioners for permission to build kilns for the roasting of limestone to make quick lime and slaked lime. This was to be both for use on the island and for sale for use on the mainland. Selby also proposed the building of a jetty and suggested that the carriage of the limestone or lime could be facilitated by the building of *'a railway'*. On 2nd August, 1845 the *Berwick Advertiser* referred to the construction of kilns at Lower Kennedy and the building of 'a roadway' to the kilns. In 1846 Selby leased the quarrying and mining rights to a local partnership formed between John Lumsden, of Mousen, and David Gibson, of Belford on the mainland, operating under the name of 'Lumsden, Gibson & Co. (Limeburners)'. Gibson was already a successful business man in Belford. He had a store from which he sold saddlery and gloves, ironmongery and groceries. He also supplied powder for blasting, shot and furniture! By 1855 Lumsden appears to have been replaced by a Mr Thomas as the company was, by then, known as Thomas, Gibson & Co. (Limeburners). It is during the lease periods of these concerns that the first waggonways were built as well as two 'capacious limekilns'. Its limeworks was known as St Cuthbert's Limeworks and was located on the Links to the north of Holy Island village.

The lime was quarried initially from the Acre limestone beds located adjacent to the seashore a short distance to the west of Snipe Point on the north side of the island. Later Coves Quarry was developed at Snipe Point. A waggonway, with several branches at the seaward end, was laid from these points in a southerly direction towards the limeworks. A low embankment allowed the lime to be tipped directly into the kilns. After roasting, the lime was removed from the kilns and spread out on a 'slaking floor' where water from a nearby well was added, converting the quick lime into slaked lime. From here some of the lime was taken by cart for 'sweetening' the soils on the island. Most was taken by waggons along a southerly continuation of the line, past Chare Ends, towards a wooden jetty which had been constructed at the 'Basin' to the west of Holy Island village. Here the lime was tipped into vessels for export to Scotland or to ports further down the Northumberland coast. The coal, for roasting the lime, was unloaded from vessels at the same jetty and transported in the waggons along the waggonway to the top of the kilns. A total of about eight men is shown in the 1851 census as being associated with the Island's lime industry at that time. Soon after this time the rail system was extended with the building of a new line linking the good quality limestone of Nessend Cliffs with the St Cuthbert's works. However, the quarrying and limeburning was soon to pass from the local consortium to 'outsiders'.

This picture is a reproduction of a painting, by artist Ralph Hedley who visited the island in the 1860s or 1870s, entitled 'Unloading coal at a wood jetty - Holy Island'. The coal is being loaded into a small, narrow gauge 'tipper' for transport to the Castle Point kilns.

Ralph Hedley, reproduced by permission of Stephenson Clarke Shipping Ltd

4 - The Nessend Quarry to Lower Kennedy Limeworks Waggonway

By 1861 there had been a rapid expansion in the lime industry as some 35 men were by then employed, many of whom originated in Scotland or Ireland. By this time the site of the winning of lime had entirely moved from the exposed seashore and low cliffs of Coves Quarry, to Nessend Quarry. This was located to the east and slightly inland from the sea cliffs at Coves Haven. Snipe Point and Coves Haven were very exposed to north easterly gales and high tides and the move to the more sheltered Nessend Quarry was seen to be thoroughly advantageous.

This expansion in the lime industry in the late 1850s and early 1860s can be ascribed to the appearance on the scene of William Nicoll of Dundee. Nicoll, born in Scotland in 1814, had been a 'Lime Merchant' for at least 20 years when he became connected with Holy Island. He signed a 25-year lease agreement with Selby in the autumn of 1858 whereby he would pay £250 as an annual rent plus a royalty of 2*d*. per ton for all lime made. Nicoll set about building a new kiln bank with three 'pots' a short distance to the south east of St Cuthbert's Limeworks. This became known as the Lower Kennedy Limeworks. Nicoll created a line from Nessend Quarry which led to the top of his new kilns. This involved the construction of a large embankment with a gentle gradient to facilitate the work of the horses hauling the loaded wagons to charge the three 'pots'. A line of rails from the quarry was retained along the base of this curved embankment to allow wagons of incoming coal from the jetty to be taken, after a reversal of direction, to the kiln-top. Roasted and slaked lime was taken to the jetty at the Basin along this line.

However, Nicoll appears to have acted precipitously, for, in 1860, a visiting Inspector of Lands reported that the kilns had been built at this point in error, and that it would be necessary for them to be abandoned. Nicoll thus relinquished these kilns (which had cost him several hundred pounds to build) and set about the construction of new, larger, kilns to the east of Holy Island Castle on the south side of the island, not far from Castle Point. To link the quarry and kilns it was necessary to construct a new line on the east side of the Island (by now usually referred to as a 'tramway'). In addition it was necessary to make new tramways, firstly to take the roasted and slaked lime from the base of the kilns to a new jetty, and secondly to bring coal from the new jetty to the top of the kilns. The former lines and the old jetty at the Basin, south of Chare Ends, were abandoned.

5 - The Nessend Quarry to Castle Point Limeworks and Lime Jetty Tramway

The eastern 'tramway', as it was now usually called, left Nessend Quarry on an incline before reversing its direction and passing through the Links (an area of dunes and loose sand). It then followed the east coast of the island heading southwards past the Lough, Holy Island's only lake. There is evidence of a double track at one point, presumably a siding or passing loop. The line then traversed a substantial embankment and crossed its only bridge. Near the base of the castle bluff a reversal was needed to allow the wagons to be hauled the

This is another Peter Westley drawing, this time of the bank of kilns at Castle Point Limeworks. As well as lines leading to the tops of the kilns there were lines leading from the kilns allowing the roasted lime to be taken, via the tramway, to the jetty for loading into sea-going vessels.
Peter Westley

This is a view of the Limeworks, below Lindisfarne Castle taken from the shore near Castle Point. The kiln had six 'pots' and is now under the protection of The National Trust who have provided an information board for the general public. *Author*

The jetty near Lindisfarne Castle survived for many years after the cessation of lime working on the Island, though gradually falling into disrepair. This picture postcard view dates from the start of the 20th century. *Author's Collection*

The present owner of this painting by artist Ralph Hedley, Fred Hoult, has very kindly agreed to allow its reproduction here. It shows the jetty, or more correctly the jetties, below Lindisfarne Castle with some laden wagons of lime about to be emptied into the hold of a waiting sailing vessel. The tide is out revealing detail of both the jetty and the vessel. *Ralph Hedley, Fred Hoult Collection*

A few vertical timbers from the lime jetty, and some mooring rings, attached to the nearby rocks, survive below the castle at the start of the 21st century. The route of the former tramway passed from the jetty, along the north side of the castle mound, towards the limeworks.

Author

Two sources reveal that William Nicoll trialled a steam locomotive on the eastern line. The identity of this locomotive has not yet been discovered. However artist Peter Westley has represented a possible scene as a train of tubs, laden with limestone, crosses the bridge and approaches the Castle Point limeworks. In the 21st century a successor to this bridge allows the former embankment to be used as a footpath from the Castle. *Peter Westley*

last few yards to the kiln top. Coal, unloaded at the new jetty, was hauled along a line which climbed and curved around the base of the castle bluff to gain the top of the kilns. Finally a line from the sidings at the base of the kilns passed beneath the bridge carrying the easterly line before following an almost level route towards the new jetty. At the approach to the jetty there were several sidings to accommodate wagons of lime awaiting shipment or to hold empty wagons awaiting loads of coal.

Horses undoubtedly provided most of the motive power for the line, though wagons were probably manhandled in the quarry and on the kiln top. However, there is the probability that a small locomotive may have been tried out on the line for a short time. A visiting Inspector Commander of the Berwick Coastguard Division (called Herbert Meritt) reported, in a letter of April 1867 to the Board of Trade, that the limestone was '...conveyed by steam engine on a line of rails a distance of two miles and burnt in lime kilns at the foot of Holy Island Castle...' Until recently this was the only suggestion that a steam locomotive had been used on the island. However, the author was telephoned by the former island postmaster, Ian McGregor, now unfortunately deceased, regarding a conversation he had enjoyed with an elderly visitor to his post office. This gentleman, also now deceased, had explained that, in the 19th century, his grandfather had driven a steam locomotive on the island for a short time. He related that its use had not been at all satisfactory as it kept leaving the rails and the line had thus reverted to the horse-haulage of wagons. Despite various enquiries the identity of this locomotive has not been discovered. Presumably it was transported to and from the island by sea.

The 'jetty' close to the castle, in reality two jetties of slightly differing heights, allowed a maximum of three vessels to be tied up at any one time. Several vessels, some of which were owned by Nicoll, took away the lime to Dundee, and travelled from there to Tyneside, where each picked up a load of coal for Holy Island. A variety of ketches, sloops, schooners and brigs were employed up to a maximum displacement of 300 tons. Vessels calling in connection with the lime trade included Nicoll's own ships, the *Marmount*, *Archduke*, *Belford* and *Robert Hood*, which had been involved, in earlier years, with the shipping of lime from Seahouses. Others included the *Agnes*, *Lancaster* and *Margaret Reid*. In coastguard records the jetty was usually referred to as the 'Lime Jetty'.

The success of the lime industry caused the island's population to rise from a figure of 497 in 1841 to 553 in 1851 reaching a peak of 622 in 1881. After the demise of the lime industry in the early 1880s the population declined rapidly, to just 444 in 1891. The last recorded cargo of lime left Holy Island lime jetty on 17th September, 1883. On 8th January, 1884 a vessel left with unspecified 'Goods' for Dundee; it is presumed that this ship was taking the last of Nicoll's remaining plant and records back to his home port. The reasons for the decline and cessation of the industry can be attributed partly to some competition from other ports (able to accommodate larger vessels) and partly to Nicoll's inability to get on with the new Estate Proprietor, Mr Robert Crossman, with whom the negotiation of a new lease would have been necessary.

The cessation of the lime industry in the early 1880s, and the relative remoteness of the Island, makes the likelihood of photographic evidence of the industry and its rail lines most unlikely. However, it is fortunate that visits were made by the artist Ralph Hedley. Two of his paintings, show the lime jetty by Lindisfarne castle. One shows the unloading of coal whilst the other shows lime being loaded onto a vessel. The paintings, which are detailed rather than impressionistic, confirm measurements from surviving wooden sleepers, that the gauge of the line was about two feet. The wagons, shown in both pictures, were of the tipping variety with wooden sides supported by metal strapping; each had four six-spoked metal wheels. In each case a horse is shown with a 'train' of one or two wagons, a suitable load bearing in mind the gradients involved. Photographs taken some 20 years after the end of commercial lime working show vessels tied up at the jetty and some evidence of the 'fan' of tracks at its approach.

Today it is possible to see the remains of the lime jetty and the iron rings to which the vessels' ropes were tied. It is also possible to follow the route of the former lines around and onto the castle mound. Then, on the east side of Lindisfarne castle one can inspect the kilns and then walk along the embankment, crossing the bridge (now rebuilt) to follow the route of the eastern tramway line. Finally, after a scramble across the sand dunes, it is possible to reach the Nessend Quarry where it is still possible to deduce some of the former rail layout. Some evidence of sleepers remains near to the quarry as do some stone blocks at the mid-point of the line which were used to stop the rails shifting when strong winds blew away sand and ballast. All of the buildings associated with the quarry (stables and houses for the workers) have disappeared. The former line to Lower Kennedy can largely be followed though the shifting dunes and the remains of the kilns at both the Lower Kennedy and St Cuthbert's works, with their associated embankments and slaking floors, can be seen. The line of the early wagonway can be followed, alongside the field boundary, from here towards the modern road to the Island which is crossed at Chare Ends, close to the new car park. Beyond here, the former trackbed crosses a private field but a short walk along the beach allows inspection of the first jetty site. A few timbers survived until recently but, as with the kilns at the St Cuthbert's and Lower Kennedy sites some vandalism has occurred. The weather and tides have also contributed to some of the industry's remains disappearing! Fortunately the kilns and surrounding land are now, like the Castle, under the protection of the National Trust, which has recently erected new information boards for the public by the kilns. If time is available it is well worth making a visit to the Island's Heritage Centre in Marygate in the centre of Holy Island's village. Here, in addition to information about the Lindisfarne Gospels, fishing industry and natural history, there are display boards relating to the Island's 'limestone past'.

Finally some words of caution. Visitors to Holy Island by car, or especially on foot, should brief themselves carefully before their visit. For several hours either side of high tide the causeway to the island becomes impassable, being covered with deep tidal water. Information in local newspapers, in tourist information centres and on noticeboards adjacent to the causeway provides information on safe crossing times. Despite this vehicles are regularly trapped by the rising tide!

Chapter Four

The Limestone Waggonways at Seahouses and Beadnell

Today the principal industry associated with the harbours of Seahouses (formerly North Sunderland Seahouses) and Beadnell is tourism. The former is the starting point for the popular boat trips to the Farne Islands where visitors can experience the excitement of being in close proximity to Britain's largest grey seal colony and to large populations of seabirds, including puffins, guillemots, cormorants and gulls. There is a small residual fishing industry. The closure of the former independent North Sunderland Railway, and the subsequent development of its land into a large car and coach park, has encouraged a large number of visitors for whom various seafood restaurants and cafes have opened. To the north is a long and beautiful beach, backed by huge dunes, which stretches from Seahouses to Bamburgh with its imposing castle. For most visitors the huge limekilns, situated overlooking the harbour, are probably of only passing interest, yet they represent the remains of an extensive lime industry which was largely responsible for the early development of Seahouses.

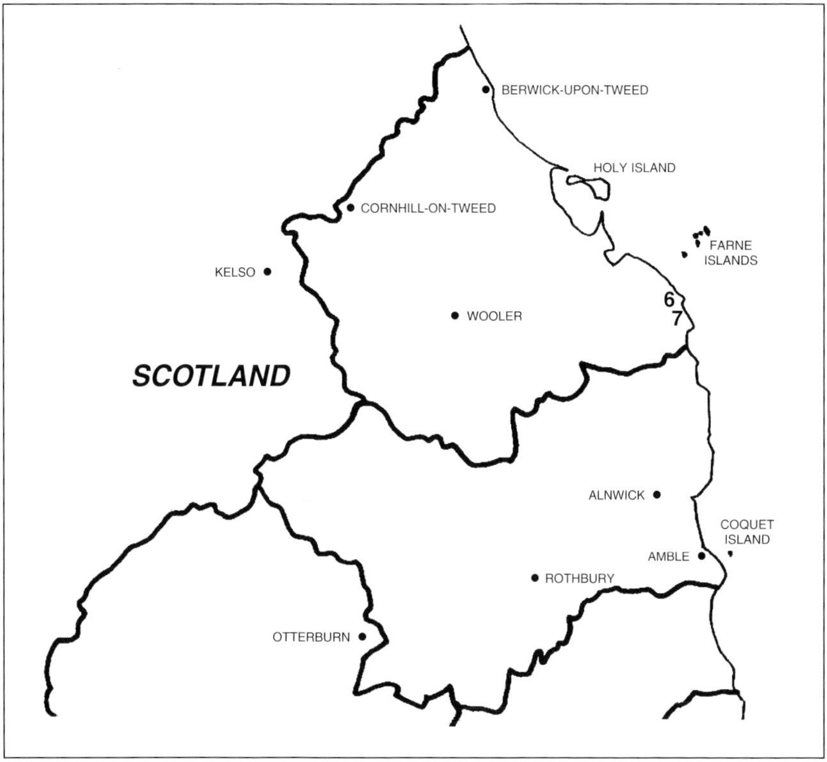

Above: Part of the western end of Seahouses limestone quarry can be seen from the side of the Seahouses to Beadnell road, not far away from the Seahouses Golf Club building. Despite the flooding the stone face can be seen on the south side.
Author

Right: The course of part of the Seahouses Tramway across the Seahouses Golf Course is readily recognisable nearly 200 years after it closed, as it ran on an embankment which raised the trackbed above the surrounding land which can become waterlogged in winter.
Author

Beadnell, a few miles to the south, is a much quieter place though in recent years, despite some opposition, it has expanded greatly due to the building of housing developments to a large extent occupied by residents who commute to work in Alnwick and Berwick. Its harbour is used largely by visitors for the launching of boats, though a very small amount of fishing still takes place. To the south of Beadnell is the large dune-backed Embleton Bay, stretching towards Dunstanburgh Castle, with its fine sandy beach. A large car park has been created behind the sand dunes a short distance from the lime kilns which dominate the small harbour. This harbour is not scoured by the tides and has always needed some dredging to allow boats of any size to enter and leave. As a result it could not compete successfully with the harbours at Seahouses and Holy Island, and its lime industry was an early casualty, soon after the start of the 19th century.

Fortunately, at both Seahouses and Beadnell, information boards have been erected to inform the public of the limestone industry associated with these ports and at the former, one of the 'stopping points' on the village walk for tourists is by the kilns at the side of the harbour.

6 - The North Sunderland Seahouses Waggonways

The industrial history of North Sunderland Seahouses (now generally called 'Seahouses') may be said to have begun in 1767 with the granting of a lease to John Pringle and James Blackett allowing them to operate coal mines and quarry lime commercially. Until this time both the winning of coal and lime had been on a small scale and for local purposes only.

The lease to Pringle and Blackett was drawn up by the local landowners, the Lord Crewe Trustees. The lease came into effect in 1768. It granted permission for the quarrying of lime (in places 24 feet thick) south of the North Sunderland Seahouses village at North Sunderland Snook (otherwise known as North Sunderland Point). It also allowed the local coal seams to be mined for fuel and permitted the erection of limekilns. The end-products were allowed to be shipped to other parts of the country from the small harbour. The lease contained provision for the construction of waggonways leading to the kilns. The enterprise was started very quickly after the granting of the lease, for, later in 1768, the coal pits were inspected by a viewer and colliery inspector, William Brown. His report found two pits working, with, nearby, some older pits which were either filled in or full of water. The pits were quite extensive (possibly indicating earlier coal extraction). One of the collieries had a shaft extending inland from the cliff face, being 400 yards-long. The coal seam being exploited was variously described as the 'Snook Top Seam' or the 'Beadnell Coal'.

Before this time the harbour at Seahouses was little more than a sandy creek. First a 'short pier' was built, then a 'long pier' (the 'middle pier' of the present harbour). These piers enclosed what is known today as the Inner Harbour. An architect called Crawmond is believed to have been associated with these works.

On 20th August, 1772 the Lord Crewe Trustees passed a resolution which included reference to both piers, which were thus in existence by that date. The

The tramway alignment, now beneath the metalled driveway, headed for the gap between the buildings on the far side of the Beadnell Road (now the B1340, King Street). The long building on the right, formerly a granary, faces in the opposite direction to the others, away from this road. The tramway originally passed in front of this building, that is, on its far side. *Author*

The tramway approach to the kilns now forms the approach drive to the Bamburgh Castle Hotel on the east side of the village square in Seahouses village. *Author*

resolution was to establish *new* 'Draw Kilns' at the harbour. The exact location of Pringle and Blackett's original kiln, or kilns, has not been identified, nor has the date when they were replaced by the new kilns. Small houses around the harbour housed the kiln workers.

The trustees granted a lease to a certain John Robinson of North Sunderland Colliery in 1797. This permitted him to take away coal but *not* lime. He was permitted to use 'barrow ways' in this connection. He obtained a further lease on 25th November, 1800 which permitted the quarrying of lime also. These dates appear to be somewhat in conflict with the oft-quoted dates of 1797-1858 for the operation of the kilns at Seahouses. Certainly the older kilns of Pringle and Blackett were in use well before 1797 whilst the newer, sandstone-built kilns were, according to this evidence, not used by Robinson until 1800 or later.

Andrew Craig Rutter, in *A Seahouses Saga* refers to the *owners* of the quarries, in 1814, as Robson and Skelly. It is, perhaps, more likely that they were lessees in view of the details of subsequent leases, which were possibly renewals.

The route of the early waggonways can be determined from several documents including the first edition Ordnance Survey maps. The earliest line ran from pits and a quarry at The Snook in the direction of the Beadnell road (now King Street) not far from what is now the clubhouse of the local golf club. Its precise year of construction has not been confirmed. However, the waggonway (or 'Railway' as it appeared on Greenwood's map of 1828) crossed the road and ran to the west of the Granary (in a shallow cutting) before heading northwards towards the harbour. At different times there were 'sidings' serving various quarry faces. The first edition OS map shows inclines and cuttings, which were probably linked with the waggonway extending from the line in a southerly direction towards the south-western extremity of a quarry close to what is now Staple Court, also to a point just to the east of the present-day alignment of the Beadnell road (now the B1340) and towards the Snook. The fields crossed by the waggonway included those known as Haggett Wells, Ramparts, Stone Close and North Kippy Law. The gauge of the line is not known but it was almost certainly narrow. It has been recorded that the wagons were pulled by Galloway horses.

On 31st August, 1829 a Lease was granted to Richard Robson and John Skelly by the Reverend Tatham and others (believed to be the Lord Crewe Trustees) to use a coal mine, erect engines and pits and borings at the collieries and to work the limestone quarries. Permission was granted,

> … to make roads, waggonways, inclined planes and other kinds of ways from the said limestone quarries to the said limekilns and also from the said colliery to the said limekilns not being through any garden or plantation … [Also they were allowed to make use of] … tubs and barrows …

This, together with the absence of the line on Greenwood's map, published in 1828, implies the construction of the second waggonway known to have existed at North Sunderland Seahouses, namely that laid between the colliery known as North Engine Pit and the kilns at the harbour. This pit was located just to the west of the road ('St Aidans') leading from Seahouses along the coast towards

Above: This photograph provides a panoramic view of Seahouses harbour at low tide with the Bamburgh Castle Hotel above the lime kilns and the RNLI lifeboat station and buildings on the right. A variety of fishing boats are seen in the harbour.

Author's Collection

Right: Two local fishermen lean on their catch boxes and converse next to the open door of their equipment store which makes use of the former lime kiln at Seahouses harbour.

Author

Bamburgh. Specifically the colliery site was situated in the fork of the present-day Broad Lane and St Aidans. (The site is marked as 'Old Colliery' on the first edition OS map and a portion of the alignment of the waggonway is marked as 'Old Tramway'; the line is shown as starting adjacent to the main colliery buildings though no sidings are shown.) The rest of the route, followed by the waggons of coal on their way to the kilns, is mostly now hidden beneath the surface of St Aidans and Seafield Road, though formerly, when the road was slightly narrower, the tramway was on a small embankment on the road's north-east side. Close to the present-day war memorial this waggonway curved to the left to gain access to the kiln tops.

The 1830s and early 1840s are usually regarded as the 'heyday' of the lime industry at Seahouses and the enterprise of Robson and Skelly was very successful. Ships laden with lime were leaving the harbour almost every day. Known destinations for the lime were Perth, Aberdeen, Blyth, Arbroath, Findhorn, Cresswell, Amble and Eyemouth. Shipments are also known to have taken place regularly to Dundee on behalf of William Nicoll (later to be associated with the lime industry on Holy Island). There was also a considerable landsale trade: loads taken by cart to Budle, Ellingham Hall, Warenford, Twizell House, Bamburgh, Newham, Alnwick, Belford, Embleton and Newton Barns are all recorded.

The names of many of the vessels involved in the export of the lime from the harbour are known. They include the *Rachel* (a sloop of 32 tons), *Marmount*, *Archduke* (a sloop of 68 tons), *Hannah*, *Hotspur*, *Johns*, *Mary Scott*, *Fender*, *Unicorn*, *Thomas*, *Jane*, *Robert Hood* (a sloop of 35 tons) and in later years the *Belford* (a schooner of 90 tons). Several of these were owned by Nicoll including the *Marmount*, *Archduke*, *Belford* and *Robert Hood*.

John Skelly is known to have died in 1843 and this may have been the reason for the advertisements which appeared in the local newspapers:

Landsale Colliery, North Sunderland
Available on 21 year lease from Bamburgh Castle.
3 pits: one engine pit (18 fathoms, 28 horsepower engine),
two coal pits, one close to engine pit, one ¼ mile away.
Coals drawn up by horse and gin.
Underground use of tubs, man hauled.
Dated May 1844

Also:

North Sunderland Limeworks
The Farm, Colliery and Limeworks at North Sunderland as at present occupied.
To be let and entered into from 11th Day of November 1844.
For further particulars apply to Mr Smeddle,
Bamburgh Castle, Belford.
Dated 3rd November, 1844.

Other records add further details to the description of the three pits at North Sunderland. The North Engine Pit was obtaining coal from the Beadnell seam. As mentioned in the advertisement this pit was 18 fathoms in depth (108 ft) and

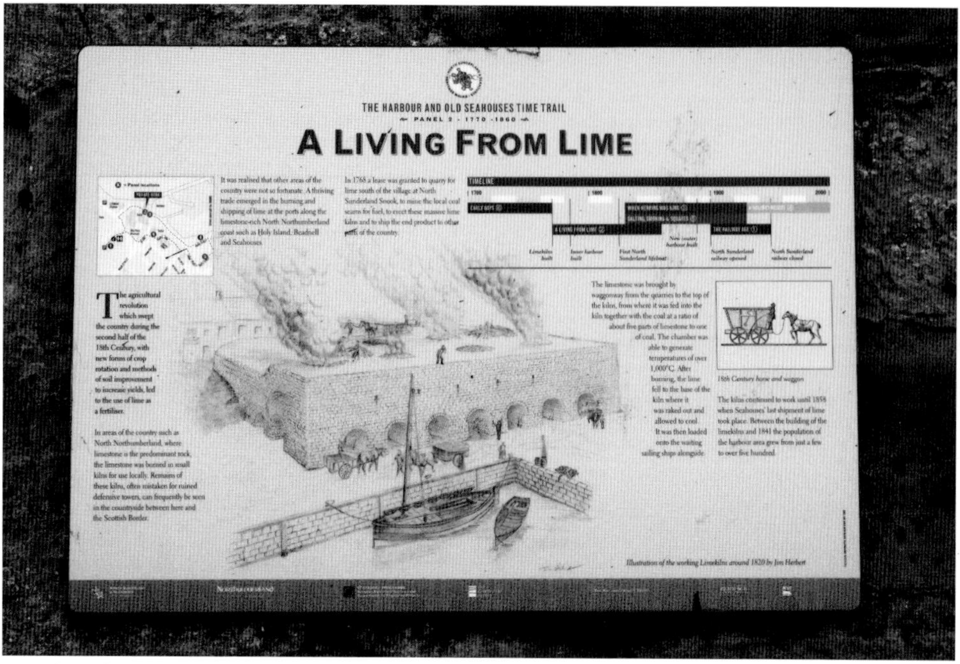

The information board on the side of the kilns at the harbour forms part of a local 'time trail' describing the history of the harbour and the surrounding area of Seahouses. *Author*

The approach road to a new housing development provides a reminder of one of Seahouses' former industries. *Author*

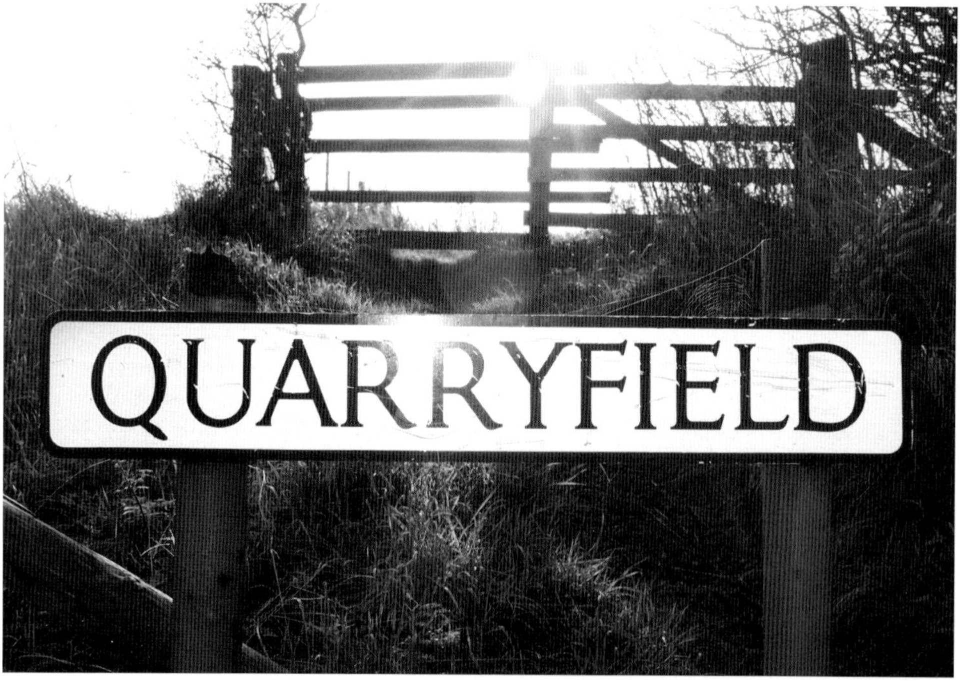

had a 28 horse power condensing engine. This removed 28 gallons of water per stroke operating at a rate of 12 strokes per minute. It worked for 12 hours each day to keep the pit dry. A horse gin was used to raise the coal to the surface. The two other pits were close to North Engine Pit. These also used horse gins to raise the coal, each requiring a horse and gin driver. The seam was a maximum of 5 ft 5½ in. in thickness. Twelve hewers and 12 putters were employed in total with a system of horse-hauled tubs taking the winnings from the coalface to the pit opening. Some of the coal from these pits was for landsale.

The 11th November lease, referred to in the advertisement, was taken up by Richard Robson and the business carried on much as before Skelly's death, the permission granting use of the colliery and mines, erection of engines and pits, borings and use of the limestone quarries. As regards the railways (for this is how they were now described in documents) and inclined planes payment of compensation was required for their use and it was required to '…embank and lay up the same...'. Various other persons were associated with Robson in the management of the enterprise. Between February 1843 and 1847 the business shipped '…4,000 loads of lime, also 5,188 loads of lime [was this 'raw' limestone or lime of a different quality?] and 40,000 bolls of coal…'.

In the 1850s the North Sunderland lime industry entered a terminal decline. Nicoll had erected his first, then his second lime works on Holy Island and his ships served there rather than the harbour at North Sunderland Seahouses. The last lime roasted at Seahouses, and coal from the nearby collieries, supplied local demands only. The number of men employed at the quarries, kilns and pits declined and the works, now becoming dilapidated and unprofitable, closed in 1858. The colliery plant was sold. One new pit was briefly established at the Snook for landsale purposes, an advertisement in the *Berwick Advertiser* asking for 10 pitmen hewers and six putters. Some of the other men found employment in the fishing industry and in carting fish to the main railway line which, with its speedy trains, had opened up new markets for the fish in the south. Ultimately Seahouses was to gain, and then lose, a railway branch of its own, the privately owned and operated North Sunderland Railway which provided a link with the East Coast main line at Chathill. This line, too 'major' for this book, has been described fully elsewhere (*see the Bibliography*).

Today parts of the former limestone quarries are filled with water and provide small havens for wildlife. Much evidence remains near the Snook of the quarrying sites and the trackbed and sidings of the first waggonway. The route of this waggonway has determined the alignment of the ends of the gardens of the present-day Mayfield and Crumstone roads. It is also responsible for the present-day, almost triangular shape, of the 'Square' at Seahouses, the rails formerly passing in front of what are now the National Trust shop and the Bank, before curving eastwards towards the kiln top. Until the 1960s there was a gap between the buildings on the south-east side of the square through which the tramway originally ran.

At the harbour-side an information board, erected on the now-protected kilns, exists to inform visitors of the now long-gone limestone industry.

Pringle's lime kiln at Benthall to the east of Beadnell village is now in a state of dereliction and may not survive for many more years if new housing continues to encroach on the surrounding fields. A coal pit lay just a few yards away, whilst the limestone quarry lay a hundred yards to the east.
Author

This photograph, taken in Autumn 2011 from between two houses in Longstone Close, shows the remains of the former Benthall Quarry which supplied the limestone for Beadnell's kilns. It is now flooded and only the tops of the stone faces can be seen. It is now almost surrounded by new housing developments.
Author

7 - The Beadnell Waggonway

Beadnell is situated to the south of Seahouses and North Sunderland on the Northumberland coast, some ten miles north-north-east of Alnwick. Its harbour is very sheltered, reputedly being the only harbour on the east coast of England to face west, away from the north-east wind!

The earliest written records of coal mining and limeburning in the area date from the first half of the 18th century, though in 1994 the remains of a mediaeval limekiln was discovered at Ebb's Neuk (or Nook) Point. Records show that the seams of 'Beadnell' or 'North Sunderland' limestone were up to 24 inches in thickness and located beneath seams of workable coal. The coal seams (the 'Beadnell Coals') were of variable thickness but reached a thickness of up to 3 ft in places.

A local man, Thomas Wood, began lime quarrying towards the end of the first half of the 18th century. He started quarrying at a headland close to the sea which became known as 'Delf Point' (sometimes recorded as 'Dell Point', 'Delves Point' or 'Delve Point'). (The word delf derives from the Old English 'delfan' meaning to dig or burrow deeply.) The nearby Beadnell coal pits, near to Ebbs Neuk, supplied the necessary coal for limeburning as well as domestic 'landsale' coal for the local inhabitants. They were in operation by 1759 and employed a windmill as a source of power, probably to power a water pump.

On 20th October, 1747 a lease between Wood and George Turnbull of Cambois, Northumberland, came into effect, with a Job Bulman acting as witness to the agreement. Turnbull was allowed to quarry for lime, to burn it, to convey the burned lime by sea and to build any buildings necessary for the work. (There was no mention, in the lease, of permission being granted for the building of waggonways or tramways, a clause which featured in many later contracts!) In practice four draw-kilns had been erected by 1759 at Delf Point, around which there is still evidence of the quarrying. The lease was to last for 30 years and Wood was to make about £100 per year from the enterprise. Turnbull was also allowed to cut away whinstone rock so as to improve the local harbour for vessels taking away his lime. Turnbull had problems, however. His kilns had been constructed near to the sea edge and on occasions the sea broke in and harmed the kilns. Turnbull abandoned the enterprise. A delightful map, drawn by James Robertson of Alnwick and dated 1759, shows the extent of the Wood Estate.

In 1759 two new coal shafts were sunk to the east of Beadnell village and by 1762 James Scott and Richard Short were described as 'pitmen'. In 1764 Wood leased to Alexander Long of 'Sherness' all of the coal mines on the south links, By the same date a lease allowed Job Bulman to ship limestone from the 'Whinstone Rock', presumably a local promontory.

In 1767 Thomas Wood died and his son, John, assumed his business interests. He clearly had no shortage of money for he bought Beadnell Hall and another local property from Richard Grieve of Alnwick, described as being '... the best two places in the village'. Various individuals, including the Archbolds of Belford and William Forster of Maryport showed interest in the local quarrying. Despite this, quarrying and limeburning became intermittent.

Right: The narrow gauge Beadnell waggonway or tramway (for it is referred to in both terms) ran from the limestone quarry to the kilns at Beadnell Harbour, following a route close to the coastline. Here it approaches the kiln top on a sharp gradient.

Author

Below: A storm is brewing in this photograph of Beadnell limekilns taken from the beach at low tide. The approach embankment is on the right-hand side.

Author

In 1796 Wood began construction of a harbour. Then in 1798 Wood leased to Richard Pringle (in a lease dated 23rd November) the nearby coal and limestone quarries. This was the start of a 20-year period when the lime industry was to function on an industrial scale. The lease, to last for 15 years, empowered Pringle to develop 'coal and limestone quarries' and to build a kiln at Benthall measuring 24 ft in diameter externally, internally tapering from 16 ft diameter at the top to 9 ft diameter at the bottom (NU236285). A coal pit was dug just a few yards from the kiln. Pringle would be allowed the profit from the burning of 4,000 loads of lime (a load being defined as 24 Winchester barrels). In addition he would pay for any damage to land as a result of his working of the coals and quarries.

Wood agreed to complete the harbour and maintain it in good repair. He approached Robert Cramond of Sunderland with a view to the construction of a new harbour at Ebbs Nook but the estimate of £8,395 was considered too expensive. Cramond also provided an estimate for a jetty at £2,942; this was also not proceeded with. Despite this Pringle exported lime by sea to ports on the east side of both England and Scotland. It must be realised that, at this time, Beadnell was a rather remote and isolated village, the road to Alnwick being a sandy track along the links and the road leading inland to Swinhoe being a turf cartway, unsuitable for the movement of heavy carts of lime. The lime trade was so good that a second and third kiln were constructed at the site. In addition a small waggonway or tramway was constructed to bring both coal and lime to the top of the kilns, one wagonload of locally mined coal being used to roast two wagonloads of limestone. The first edition OS maps show most of the course of the tramway. It started from the quarries at 'The Benty' and followed the coastline to the east of what is now Harbour Road (NU235290). Much of the route was on a small embankment. The last part of its route can still be followed today, partly as a public footpath, as it leads towards the tops of the kilns, though a recently erected barrier prevents access to the kiln tops for safety reasons.. The precise gauge of the line has not been recorded but it was certainly 'narrow', probably in the region of 2 ft. The line was almost half a mile in length. Horses provided the motive power and a blacksmith's forge was located nearby.

Despite the initial optimism and success, the lime industry was to last barely 20 years. By 1818 the kilns were out of use and in 1822 Wood gave permission for them to be used for fish curing. In 1827 Thomas Hill (a cooper of Berwick) and John Ormston (a former customs officer) built herring yards next to the kilns. By the same year the original Beadnell Colliery had also ceased production as one of its principal markets, the kilns, had closed. Hill and Ormston's business was to last until 1841. It is unfortunate, from a 'records' point of view, that the kilns and tramway had closed by 1818. As a result neither Fryer's nor Greenwood's maps of Northumberland (dated 1820 and 1828 respectively) show them, though the line to the kilns at Sunderland Seahouses [*sic*] was shown on Greenwood's map.

No more lime was roasted at Beadnell. The kilns at Seahouses then, later, on Holy Island taking over the coastal trade. However, attempts were made to resurrect the coal industry. In 1862 borings for coal were conducted and by the

In the immediate post-World War II era the limekilns overlook a quartet of small fishing boats in the harbour at Beadnell. It would be some years before tourism would take over from fishing as the village's major industry. Beadnell is the only harbour on the east coast of England which actually faces west! *Author's Collection*

This autumn 2011 view of the Beadnell kilns can be contrasted with the earlier photograph taken some 60 years earlier. The vessel in the harbour is one of the surviving 'cobles', a type of fishing boat unique to the Northumberland coast. This one is normally based at Craster harbour. *Author*

The draw hole of one of the 'pots' of the Beadnell kilns can just be seen behind a fisherman's stored lobster pots, rope and plastic containers. Although Beadnell's economy relies quite heavily upon tourism there are still the vestiges of the fishing industry. *Author*

1880s the colliery owner was a certain R.H. Taylor. The colliery (NU232290), under Manager R. Spence, was winning coal from a seam which varied between 2 ft 6 in. and 3 ft in thickness. In the 1890s the coal was mined by V.W. Corbett & Company though there were problems with the ingress of water. In 1896 12 men were employed at the pit and the output was exclusively household coal for landsale. There was thus no need for the use of a rail line to distribute the coal. On the 6th June, 1897 the colliery closed and coal mining at Beadnell ceased.

Today it is possible, with the aid of a large scale local map, to discover the now water-filled old limestone quarry behind the houses of Longstone Close. Just to the west, adjacent to the path leading southwards from Meadow Lane in Beadnell village, is the site of the former coal pit and the old limekilns which pre-date those at the harbour. Parts of the route of the waggonway can be followed as it hugged the coast as it approached the kilns, though some sections have disappeared as a result of the building of 20th century houses and gardens. The kilns themselves have been repaired at different times and, as mentioned earlier, an adjacent board provides some information on Beadnell's former lime industry. Beadnell harbour is now the preserve of a few fishing boats and pleasure craft.

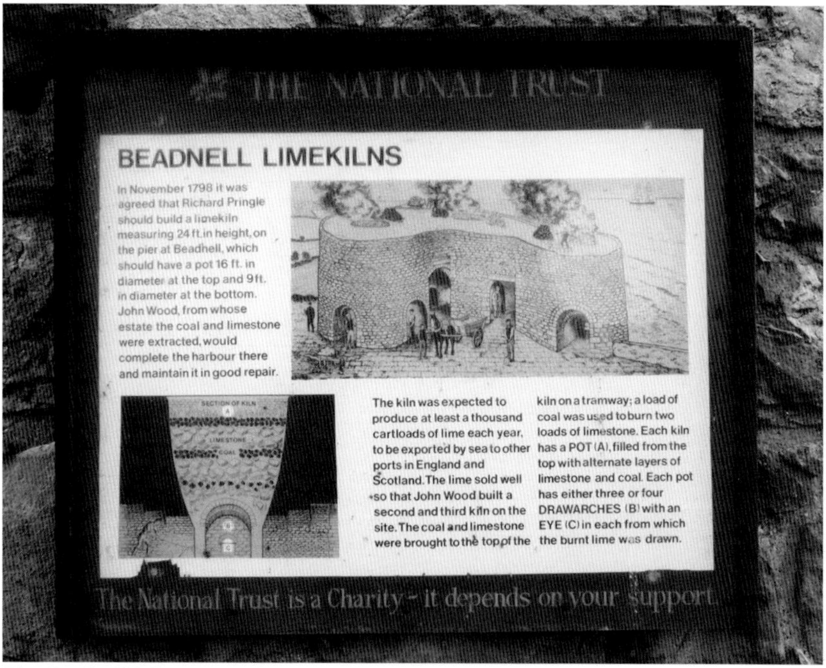

The Beadnell kilns are under the protection of the National Trust and this body has erected an information board on the side of the kilns explaining to visitors their role in the early 19th century lime industry. A diagram explains the functioning of a kiln whilst an artist has provided an impression of the working kilns. *Author*

Chapter Five

The Limestone Tramways of Ancroft and Lowick

The part of northern Northumberland from Ancroft village in the north through Berrington and Bowsden to just south of Lowick is an area possessing, according to various trade directories '... inexhaustible seams of coal and limestone ...' These two raw materials ensured that this area would become the most important lime-producing area away from the north Northumberland coast to the south of Berwick.

Lime from this locality was used for building, for agricultural purposes and as a lime wash for buildings, and was transported elsewhere, such as to sites over the Scottish border. Lime from the Ancroft area kilns was used in making the mortar used in the construction of the Royal Border Bridge to carry the main line railway over the River Tweed between Tweedmouth and Berwick. Some lime is recorded as leaving Tweedmouth by sea, probably destined for Scotland.

The limestone layers worked included the 'Acres', the 'Eelwell' and the 'Oxford' whilst the associated collieries tapped seams that were a westwards extension of the Scremerston coalfield. (As well as supplying the lime industry some coal from these pits was sold for local domestic use.) Greenwood's map of 1828 shows at least 10 kilns at work in this area and there was a similar number of collieries, some being mechanized with the employment of steam engines for pumping water and raising coal. Some limestone quarries employed small

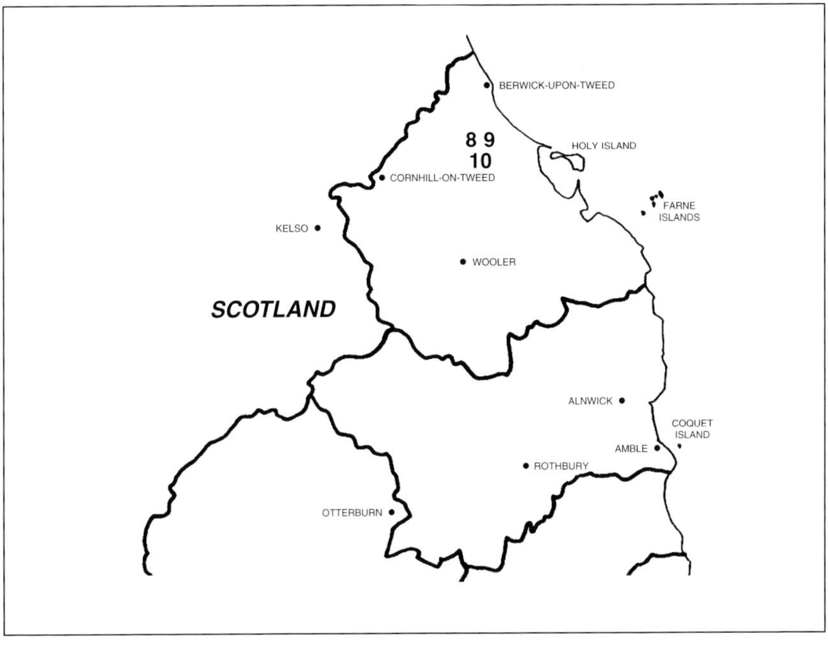

Above: The site of the kiln of Ancroft limeworks was on the small raised mound at the edge of the wood in the background. In the foreground is the slightly raised embankment of the small tramway leading from the nearby colliery. The quarries were located behind the trees and off the picture to the right.
Author

Right: This cutting led from the limestone quarry towards the Ancroft Kiln mound. The first Ordnance Survey maps identified a 'crank' at the top of this cutting perhaps identifying some type of haulage device or engine. The quarry faces were beyond the present-day trees and bushes.
Author

tramways to move the stone from the faces to the kilns; others used horse-drawn carts or manpower. Some switched between these methods. Horse-drawn carts were generally used to transport the roasted lime away from each limeworks.

Although the 19th century must be regarded as the 'heyday' of the local lime industry it was in existence much earlier. For example a 1763 advertisement relating to some property at Ancroft Green, near Ancroft, appeared in the *Newcastle Courant* newspaper: '...170 acres, a dwelling house, valuable seams of limestone 4 yards thick which will last for ages, two draw kilns from whence has been sold yearly 14,000 bolls of shell lime at 6d per boll.' The owner, Mr Sibbitt of Shoreswood, was, however, unable to effect the sale. Remarkably even as late as 13th March, 1952 the *Berwick Advertiser* contained a report that a Mr W.R. Sitwell of Barmoor Castle Estate had recommenced the opening of a quarry between Barmoor and Lowick, a quarry which had last been worked in 1893! This limestone was crushed to make a fertiliser for the fields without roasting. A contemporary Ordnance Survey map indicates a small quarry building, marked 'works' which was not present on earlier and subsequent maps, that may have been associated with this activity.

In the vicinity of Ancroft village there were five fairly substantial limestone quarries with associated kilns: Ancroft Greens (see above) to the west of the village, Ancroft North Farm (to the north), and Oxford (to the north-east), all of which had two kilns, plus Ancroftstead Limeworks to the south-east and Ancroft Limeworks (next to Ancroft Town Farm near the village centre). It is almost certain that a tramway (or wagonway) existed at Ancroft Limeworks and one may have existed at Ancroftstead. Collieries which could have supplied the necessary coal were located at Longdike, Ancroft North Farm, Ancroft Greens (otherwise called Allerdean Greens), Ancroft Stead Pit, and Ancroft Trials Pit, all close to the village.

Surviving records indicate that most of the lime, for the lime mortar used by contractors McKay & Blackstock during the building of the Royal Border Bridge, to cross the River Tweed between Tweedmouth and Berwick, was obtained from the limeworks in the Ancroft District. It was transported to the site in carts. Here 'A4' class Pacific No. 60007 heads northwards over the Royal Border Bridge with a special train. *Gareth Patterson*

Two miles south of Ancroft were the Berrington Lime Quarries and the Bowsden Quarries. Another half-mile to the south were the extensive Dryburn Quarries ('Old' and 'New') with at least three kilns operating at different locations and times. A further short distance to the south were the Lowdean Limeworks, the small Acres Quarry and the extensive Eelwell Quarries. Finally, to the south of Barmoor and the Lowick road were quarries close to Barmoor Moss. Most of these quarries were substantial in size. Coal was obtained for these from a pit near Berrington village, from Dryburn Colliery (close to the lime quarries), Lickar Colliery and Coal Pit (to the east of the Dryburn quarries), and Barmoor Colliery. The majority of these quarries and collieries were located to the side of the road leading southwards from Ancroft towards Barmoor (now part of the B6525 Berwick to Wooler road) which was used to cart away the lime. A tramway, shown on OS maps, linked Barmoor Quarry with a kiln at Dryburn. It is likely, too, according to 'handed-down' oral evidence, that there was a wagonway or tramway linking the western end of the Eelwell Quarry with a kiln at the western end of New Dryburn Quarry. Similarly there may also have been lines serving kilns within Eelwell Quarry and nearby Acres Quarry. In these cases the evidence from old maps and on-the-ground surveys is inconclusive. The smoothed gradients and small embankments may have been constructed for either tramways or cartways. A local village website has referred to them as 'wagonways'. However, primary documentary evidence has proved elusive. Most of these sites are on private land and the usual cautions apply.

Though not coming within the scope of this book as it was mooted by a 'main line' railway company, mention must be made of an 1848 proposal by the York, Newcastle & Berwick Railway. This involved a branch leaving the Newcastle to Berwick line at Beal and progressing via Barmoor to Wooler. If constructed, this line would have facilitated the transport of lime away from the kilns and quarries located between Ancroft and Lowick. The detailed plans and sections for the line are held in the Tyne and Wear Record Office in Newcastle.

8 - The Ancroft Tramways

To the west of Ancroft Town Farm and to the north of the Dean Burn lay the Ancroft Limeworks (NT996452). Its quarries were located near to the works, especially towards the south-west. The 1860 OS map indicates a likely line of tramway leading up from the quarry, via a cutting, towards a 'turntable' and a 'crank' which may have been a form of winch used to draw the wagons of lime from the quarry. Although buildings are shown at the works there is no indication as to which was the kiln so it is not possible to confirm that the turntable diverted the line towards this! One of the buildings is marked as an engine house, which could have provided power for a winch or crank. A coal pit on the Long Dike road was situated a short distance away and it is likely that this was also directly connected to the works, as early OS maps mark a 'track' leading from the pit towards the 'turntable'. By the time of the publication of the 1890s maps the works had closed. The 1920s and later editions of the OS maps still show the cutting on the likely tramway route between quarry and works sites. Contact with a local farmer brought forward the suggestion that it was worth studying the earthworks, including a small embankment, which could provide evidence for lines to the works.

Today the site of the former limeworks lies in a field owned by a local company, United Agri Products (UAP). They kindly gave permission for visits to the field which lies beyond their offices which are located in a former workman's cottage. A double gate, leading from their concreted yard close to the former coal pit site marked on the 19th century map, leads directly onto a low raised embankment, several metres wide, running towards the site of the former kiln at the far edge of the field. This raised area has slight differences in its vegetation from the surrounding areas of the field. At first this embankment is almost straight but it curves gently to the right as the works site is reached. It lies on the route between the sites of the old coal pit and the limeworks indicated on the old maps.

From the limeworks site a steep descending incline runs, mainly in a cutting, towards part of the former limestone workings. (On the occasion of one visit, after rain, this cutting was very wet and hauling up loaded wagons of stone could have been very difficult in the absence of rails.) Thick vegetation beyond the fenced field boundary and the absence of a convenient stile make investigation of the rest of this incline impossible. These observations agree closely with the 19th century map evidence and suggest that both coal and limestone could have been brought to the works by means of tramways. There are no building remains at this site visible on the surface; however some cut stones, appearing to be limestone blocks, are present on the slope in the adjacent woodland and may perhaps be building remains.

So far it has not been possible to trace any primary documents relating directly to this limeworks so as to corroborate the 'on-the-ground' and cartographic 'evidence', and thus confirm the existence of the rail lines associated with this works. However, the available evidence appears to be convincing, to the author at least!

9 - *The Dryburn Tramways*

The earliest lime workings at Dryburn took place to the east of the Lowick-Ancroft road at Old Dryburn. Several lime kilns are marked on maps, both at the time of Greenwood's survey of the early 1820s and the later Ordnance Survey maps. A number of small coal pits are marked nearby, such as that at Lickar, opened in 1854, no doubt the source of fuel for firing the kilns. (A much older pit had been operating at Lickar in the 1790s.) A multiplicity of what may have been cartways or tramways are marked linking quarry faces and kilns in Dryburn Quarry. Despite much erosion some of these can be followed at the start of the 21st century. In places the gentle inclines or gradients indicate efforts being made to facilitate the movement of coal or lime to the kiln tops, whether by means of carts or tramway wagons.

A later Dryburn kiln, at New Dryburn, to the west of the Berwick Road, appears on the first OS maps surveyed in the early 1860s. It was located on land owned by Francis Sitwell. A short distance to the north the Dryburn Colliery was active. The kiln received its limestone via a tramway from a quarry to the south of Barmoor

The embankment of the former 'Barmoor Tramway' is shown running from left to right from behind the horse, past the centrally placed bush, towards the field boundary by the tree on the right-hand side. The quarry was located some 200 yards to the right of this view across a further field. Remains in this field have been removed by the plough. *Author*

Mill (NT997404). This quarry did not appear on Greenwood's map but is already quite extensive on the first OS maps. Hence it is very likely that it was developed, and the tramway was laid, in the second quarter of the 19th century. Measurements of the width of the trackbed on the surviving lengths of tramway embankment indicate that the line was of narrow gauge, probably of about two feet.

The Barmoor Quarry itself, though supplying the New Dryburn kilns, was a western 'outpost' of the Eelwell quarries which were mainly developed to the east of the Berwick Road. In the 1860s the main quarry faces were being extended in an east-west direction. Branches of the 'Barmoor Tramway' served these faces. The quarry and tramway lines reached as far west as the field boundary level with the midpoint of the Barmoor Mill Pond 100 yards or so to the north. The line left the quarry on its northern side and climbed towards the edge of the adjacent field where it crossed the 300 ft contour line marked on the OS map. To the east of this point the quarry was barely developed. The tramway line then headed diagonally

This is the mound which was formerly the site of the New Dryburn Limeworks. The Barmoor Tramway transported lime from the Barmoor Quarry towards the works which was approached via a bridge over a local burn and an embankment. The limeworks also served the nearby Dryburn Quarries. *Author*

across the field in a north-easterly direction towards Dryburn. It crossed the field boundary marked, as it is still today, by a line of trees. Here the field sloped downwards and it was necessary to construct an embankment for the line to even out the gradient. This was constructed using a base of larger stones with smaller stones laid on top. A farm track, leading to the ford at the mill was then crossed before the field level fell away steeply towards the Dry Burn. Map evidence shows that the line became slightly elevated at this point so as to cross over the burn. The still-existing embankment ends quite abruptly and it is therefore likely that a form of wooden trestle bridge existed, though this is not identified on maps. On the far side of the burn the land rises up from the burn and the line appears to have, once again, been built on an embankment as it approached the kiln top via a right-hand curve. The embankment is not as clearly defined as that on the south side. The bank against which the kiln was created, survives today, though its edges are crumbling. The remains of the kiln have long-since been reduced to rubble. A surviving cart track leads over an old bridge spanning the Dry Burn and this would have been used by carts taking lime from the kiln base to the nearby main road. A nearby bench mark indicates an altitude of around 245 feet. Horses would have been needed to haul the wagons on the tramway, especially on the steep exit from the quarry. A smithy was located nearby at the entrance to the main Eelwell Quarry. There is no documentary evidence identifying the location of the stables though there are several outbuildings shown at the nearby Barmoor water mill.

Kelly's Directory of 1858 refers to Robert Stevenson of Lowick Northfield Farm as being a 'farmer, limeburner and colliery owner', also to Charles Salsbury resident at Red House being a 'farmer, coal owner, limeburner and brick and tile manufacturer'. In the 1850s the Manager of the Dryburn Limeworks is recorded as a certain Thomas Webster. By the mid-1880s he had been replaced by

One remarkable survivor is the old bridge which was located on the trackway which linked the base of the New Dryburn kilns to the adjacent Ancroft to Lowick Road. The bridge is made from limestone cut from one of the local quarries. The kiln was located at the top of the mound on the left hand side. Some of the uneven ground consists of overburden from the former Dryburn Quarries behind the kiln. *Author*

Adam Hills who had formerly been a labourer at the same works. A document survives in the form of a receipt, dated 23rd May, 1871, and headed 'Barmoor, Dryburn and Lowick North Limeworks'. This suggests that all of the local limeworks were, in some way, working in conjunction with each other. The census records give an indication of the extent of the lime industry in the Lowick locality: in 1851 four limestone quarrymen, one labourer and two lime carters are recorded. In 1861 there was one limeburner, five limestone miners and three limestone quarrymen. By 1871 one lime quarryman, seven lime labourers, one quarry labourer and one quarryman were recorded. (It is accepted that some of these may have been employed at other quarries or limeworks in the Lowick district). Up to 20 coalminers were employed locally.

By the time of the survey for the second edition Ordnance Survey maps the Barmoor Quarry had become more extensive. In the 30 years since the first survey it had been extended in a westerly direction about halfway across the next field and had been deepened. It had also been extended in an easterly direction back towards the main Berwick to Wooler road. It is known that the quarry closed in 1892, caused, it is reported, by an outbreak of anthrax in the local population. The second edition OS maps thus reflect the situation around the time of closure. The quarry is marked as an 'Old Quarry' both to the west and east of the tramway route, with all of the tracks within the quarry having been lifted. However, the trackbed is shown as intact from the quarry exit across the two fields, over the embankment and across the burn as far as the kiln. The coal pit at Dryburn had closed by this time and no remains are shown on the map. The nearby Acres Quarry was marked as 'Disused'.

The kiln at Old Dryburn survives today on private land and is photographed here, with permission, from the grounds of the house formerly known as 'New Dryburn', but today renamed 'Doll's House'. The growth of trees close to the kiln makes on-the-ground research difficult. *Author*

Today the site of New Dryburn kiln lies on private ground. The quarry can be approached by means of a public footpath leading through a gate from the bridge over the Dry Burn on the road to Barmoor Mill. Less than 100 yards along the footpath the remains of the tramway embankment can be seen as far as the first field boundary. Beyond this point ploughing has removed all traces. A deviation must be made, following the public footpath, to enter the next field by means of a chained gate. Following the path on the edge of this field brings you to the quarry, approached today via a short but steep path. Much of the quarry is now flooded (especially in winter) and it is not possible to follow the former rail alignments. The western end of the quarry has been partially filled in with tipped material. The footpath continues through and out of the quarry towards Barmoor village and castle, though a deviation may have to be made around the edge of the field to avoid any growing crop. On the other side of the Berwick road, towards Old Dryburn the well-preserved remains of an old kiln, located on private land, can be seen from the roadside close to the house known today as 'Doll's House', formerly as 'New Dryburn'.

10 - The Eelwell Tramways

It has been suggested locally, including on a village website, that there were early tramways or wagonways in the quarry at Eelwell, near Lowick. This quarry lies to the south of Dryburn and to the north of Lowick Northfield Farm. A sale document, relating to 'Lowick North Farm' includes reference to 'Eals Well Field' [*sic*] with a '... limestone quarry of five acres and lanes thereto and from ...' It also refers to an 'old limestone quarry' and 'old lime kiln' in a field known as 'Old Brooms'. However, no reference is made to tramways in this document. The quarry had two kilns in the 1860s, one close to the Lowick to Ancroft road served the more western parts of the quarry, whilst the other, to the east, served the rest of the quarry. A smithy was located adjacent to the Lowick-Ancroft road. Map evidence is inconclusive though markings may indicate a line of rails at the western end of the quarry adjacent to the smithy. Similarly at the eastern kiln a map line along the top of the kiln embankment may suggest a small tramway. In the absence of further documentary evidence the existence of these lines cannot be confirmed. As mentioned earlier, on-site research has proved to be inconclusive. There is no evidence of old rails *in situ* or in use as fences. By the 1890s the quarry was closed and disused. Today much of the former quarry has become flooded and the surrounding land has been planted with trees, obscuring possible 'on-the-ground' evidence. The site lies on private land and permission must be sought to access it.

Sitwell's detailed 1838 proposals, for a railway to link the quarries at Eelwell and kilns near to Barmoor with the Wooler to Coldstream turnpike road at Flodden have already been described (*see Volume One*). If built, this line, in addition to the movement of coal, bricks and tiles, would have provided another outlet for the lime from the Dryburn and Eelwell Quarries and kilns, towards Wooler and Coldstream. However, there is no evidence that this railway progressed beyond the planning stage.

This across-the-fields photograph, taken from the Little Mill to Alnwick road shows the former Little Mill limeworks. On the left is the second of the two limekilns, reputed to be one of the largest in the country, and on the right is the house known as 'The Limery', formerly lived in by the Richardson family that operated the works. *Author*

Photographed from the top of the second kilns at Little Mill is John Richardson's house, still lived in, and known as 'The Limery'. The area behind the barn to the left is the former limestone quarry, now a nature reserve, which can be approached via a marked footpath which starts just behind the house. *Author*

Chapter Six

Limestone Railways at Little Mill and Longhoughton Quarries

As mentioned in Volume Three in this series, there were two major quarries at Little Mill, near Littlehoughton, some 3½ miles north-east of Alnwick, namely the Little Mill Whinstone Quarry and the Little Mill Limestone Quarry. These quarries both had standard gauge sidings with connections to the main line and operated their own 'internal' narrow gauge lines. Their histories run in parallel, as, for most of their existence, they were leased to, and worked by the same companies or individuals. As a consequence some details have already appeared in the previous volume, describing the whinstone quarry, and will not be repeated here.

A further quarry, located to the west of Longhoughton village also produced limestone, though later, owing to a unique local geology, it produced large quantities of whinstone.

Above: This delightful late 19th century (or early 20th century) photograph is the only one that has been traced showing the workings within Little Mill limestone quarry. Note the wagons, the horses, the derelict-looking steam engine and what may be a pump on the skyline. The gentleman in the bowler hat is John Richardson, the quarry lessee. The lady in the long dress may well be his wife, Mary.

Author's Collection

Right: Photographed from the kiln top at the end of the approach tramway is a brick-lined pot of the first lime kiln at Little Mill. The view is taken looking north with the East Coast main line railway on the right, just out of view.

Author

11 - The Little Mill Limestone Quarry Railway

The Little Mill Limestone Quarry (sometimes spelt as one word, 'Littlemill', on maps and documents), was situated on the west side of the East Coast main line just to the south of Little Mill station (NU228174). This limestone quarry, extracted stone from the Acre seam. It is known to have been in existence in the 18th century and it served the first kiln, which was circular in outline. Coal, for roasting the lime, came from the numerous small nearby pits, such as Lea Moor Colliery (where there were two coal seams, one of 2 ft 6 in. and one of 4 ft 6 in.) and Rennington Colliery which was supplying coal to Little Mill in 1883. A trackway from Lea Moor, which headed towards the limeworks and was shown on Ordnance Survey maps for over 100 years, was probably the means by which some coal was brought to the kilns. It has been suggested that this was formerly a small tramway, though it is not marked as such on old maps and no documentary evidence has been discovered to confirm its existence. At this time the roasted lime was used principally for agricultural purposes and was taken away by horse-drawn carts to local farms.

The first, smaller, kiln was replaced by a much larger kiln with eight 'pots' in the first half of the 19th century. This 'new' kiln is amongst the largest ever to have been built in Great Britain. It still stands today, visible from trains on the adjacent East Coast main line, a testament to the quality of its construction. It was built around the time of the construction of the adjacent Newcastle & Berwick Railway (built 1845-47). This opened up the possibility, for the limeworks, of a greatly increased trade in lime with new markets being accessed via the railway. A connection between the main line and the limeworks was created soon after the railway opened, allowing both the 'export' of lime from the site and the bringing to the site of cheaper or better coal for burning the limestone. The total area of the quarry was about 4½ acres, later increased by about another half an acre when it was extended into a nearby field known as Cow Close. The first area to be quarried was close to the kilns, whilst later quarrying took place at stone faces further away.

The limeworks site lay on the Howick estate of the famous Grey family. The earliest known tenant was the mining engineer, William Barkus, born in Lumley, County Durham, who also rented the Little Mill Whinstone Quarry. Barkus took out a lease on the Little Mill limestone quarry, dated 12th May, 1848. He operated the limeworks until 1878 when his business finally collapsed and he was forced to relinquish the leases on his various quarries.

The limeworks and quarry, will, however, always be associated with the Richardson family who were limeburners at Little Mill, either as employees or tenants, for well over 100 years. The 1841 census identifies Robert Richardson (aged 48), together with his wife Mary (aged 40) and their children, John (14), Arthur (12), Margaret (10), Alice (5), Robert (3) and baby William (10 months). Robert described himself as a 'lime manufacturer'. His son, John, was described as a 'gardener'. They would, at this time, be firing the first Little Mill kiln.

By the time of the 1851 census (soon after the opening of the nearby railway) Robert was describing himself as the 'Superintendent of the Lime Works', whilst his eldest son, John (now 24), was also now linked with the works and

These two photographs, taken from the yard at the Limery, show the first kiln to be built at the site. The first picture was taken over 25 years ago whilst the second shows the present-day view.
Brewis Family Collection (above), Author (below)

described as a 'limeburner'. Some of the children had, by this time, left home and only John, Robert and William, plus the latest arrival, Thomas, were still living there. Several other residents of Little Mill and nearby Little Houghton (today usually spelt as one word) were associated with the works as limeworks labourers. Others worked in the local coal pits as miners.

By 1861 it was Robert's eldest son, John, who was 'Manager of the Limeworks' and living at 'Little Mill Limery'. In the previous 10 years he had married Mary Railston of Embleton and they were blessed with four children: Elizabeth, Mary, Robert R., and Ellen. By 1871 John's census entry described him as a 'limeburner'. Three more children had arrived, John, Alice and Laura Jane. John was ultimately to succeed his father in charge of the works.

The 1881 census records John Richardson, (by now 54) as a 'Lime Burner employing 21 men and 5 boys' and gives an indication of the success that the quarry and works was enjoying at that time. (Some secondary sources have claimed that a total of 100 men worked at the quarry. This may be the sum total of the workers at both the limestone and nearby whinstone quarries; even so it seems to be a rather large figure!) Whilst all of the daughters still lived at home, John (junior), now a young man had left home and was serving an apprenticeship at the Elswick Works in Newcastle. He qualified as a mechanical engineer, having studied and worked on marine engines and boilers. By the early 1900s John (junior) was in charge of the works but his own son John was living at Little Mill, and presumably associated with, if not working at, the works.

The 'third' John was to succeed his father in charge of the limeworks and managed it until the late 1930s, when, in turn, he was succeeded by his own son Henry (usually known as 'Harry'). Successive renewals of the lease to the Richardsons had taken place in 1902, 1931, 1939 and finally in 1949. In the late 1940s Harry was said to be more interested in farming than managing a by-now ailing limeworks (and whinstone quarry). As described in Volume Three he decided to surrender the lease on the whinstone quarry but renewed the

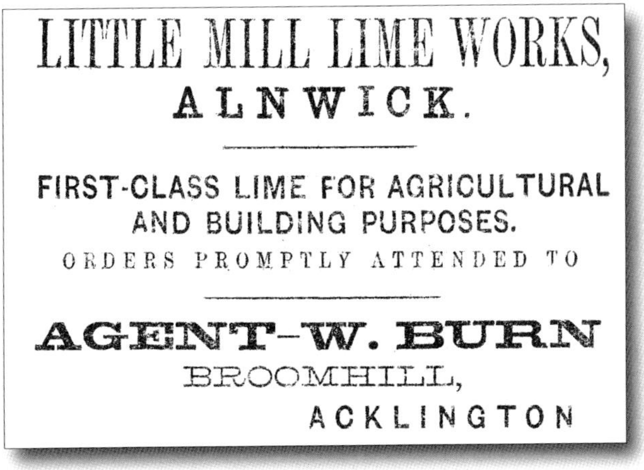
LITTLE MILL LIME WORKS,
ALNWICK.

FIRST-CLASS LIME FOR AGRICULTURAL
AND BUILDING PURPOSES.
ORDERS PROMPTLY ATTENDED TO

AGENT–W. BURN
BROOMHILL,
ACKLINGTON

This advertisement for Little Mill Lime Works appeared in several forms in various local newspapers and guides. *Author's Collection*

This plan, based on other hand-drawn documents, shows the extent of both the narrow- and standard-gauge rail system at Little Mill around the year 1900 when the new kiln bank was in use. The small building to the west of the 'Coal Depot' is probably the powder store which has survived into the 21st century. *Author*

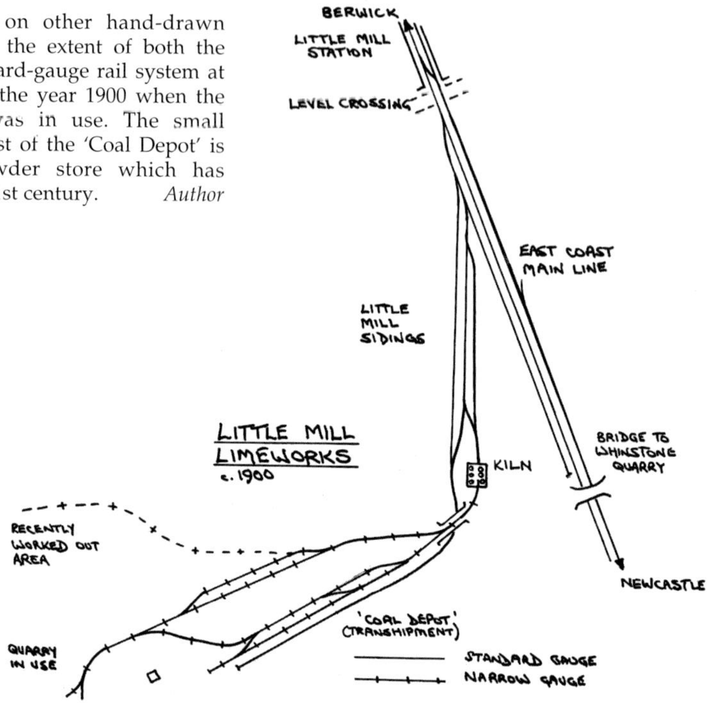

This view of the 'new' kiln at Little Mill is taken from the site of the former standard gauge sidings. Soon after this 2011 photograph was taken the kiln became encased in scaffolding as essential repairs commenced. *Author*

limeworks and quarry lease for a little longer. His father, John, was by then in poor health and Harry did not want to upset him by surrendering the limeworks lease as well. The final surrender of the lease occurred on 12th May, 1960. After this Harry continued living at the house known as 'Limery' until he died in the late 1960s.

At the start of the Richardson 'dynasty' the quarry, with a workforce numbering into the twenties, was producing around 6,000 tons of lime per year. In the 1890s the figure had fallen slightly to around 4,000 tons, which level was to be maintained until the start of World War I. At the time the ground rent paid was about £166 per annum with royalties based on the stone extracted adding about £150 to that figure annually. (This last figure was latterly reduced after negotiations between Richardson and the Howick Estates, with Richardson arguing, not for the first time, that the quarry would be unprofitable if the rent was high.)

In the early 1920s, after the end of the Great War, production increased slightly. An account book for 1923 lists destinations for the lime as including Blyth, Ashington, Ayton, Prudhoe, Lucker, Coldstream, Akeld, Morpeth, Bishop Auckland and Wooler. A typical total dispatched from the sidings was 91 tons per fortnight. Some of the lime was being sent to ironworks (such as Blyth Star Foundry and Emmerson Walker at Dunston) for use as a flux, whilst reducing quantities were being sold locally for agricultural use. Other consignments of 'raw' (that is, unroasted) limestone left the quarry. Later in the 1920s production was reported as being markedly down. John Richardson wrote to the Howick Estates (his landlords) stating that the quarry was running at a loss, quoting several contributory reasons:

- less lime was being requested by the gas company in Newcastle (a major customer) as it was changing its production methods;
- the building industry was making use of cement rather than lime mortar;
- buildings were being made of concrete, not stone and mortar;
- farmers were not using lime on their fields as they couldn't afford it;
- the rent of the quarry was too high.

He obtained his requested reduction in rent!

Earlier Richardson had complained about water problems in the quarry as a result of seepage from the old pits nearby, and also of the amount of unproductive work necessitated by a 16-17 ft layer of overburden which had to be removed before stone quarrying could begin. It was necessary at times to keep the pumps working for nine hours a day to keep the quarry dry, the pumps removing 120 gallons of water per hour. The problems of the limeworks continued with the miner's strike when coal supplies dried up. (In 1926 Richardson requested permission for the second time, the first had been in 1912, to reopen the pits on his property, drain them and extract coal. The Howick Estates once again refused permission on the grounds that that the pumped-out water, discharged into the Howick Burn, would cause pollution and discolour the water supply to Howick Hall!)

For some reason Richardson applied, in 1934, to use the accommodation bridge, originally designed for agricultural purposes, which crossed the East

The weather and grazing animals have caused most of the quarry faces at Little Mill limestone quarry to disappear. However, some of the more recently quarried faces survive at the south end of the quarry. *Author*

The routes of some of the narrow gauge lines can be followed through Little Mill quarry. Here is a junction where the line to the south quarry face left the line to the west face. *Author*

Coast main line but linked the land of the limestone and whinstone quarries. The LNER Engineer's Department at York turned the application down on the grounds that it was not strong enough to support vehicles associated with the stone trade. The purpose of this application is not clear.

Further figures to illustrate the extent of lime production are not available until those of the 1940s by which time a marked decline had set in, despite Little Mill, since 1930, being the only works firing lime in the area. Even this ceased temporarily in September 1941, to be resumed briefly a few years later. In 1944 slightly less than 700 tons had left the quarry (being made up of roasted lime and quarried limestone in equal amounts). By 1946 the total was down to only 400 tons. Despite a brief resurgence in demand, to just over 1,000 tons in 1947 and 1,700 tons in 1948, the quarry effectively closed at the end of 1948. The last stone to leave was foundry limestone and ground limestone. No stone was quarried or roasted during the 10 years or so of the lease negotiated in 1949.

The standard gauge railway sidings to serve the limeworks had been installed by the time of the survey for the first edition Ordnance Survey maps. These maps show that the sidings were approached by means of a trailing connection from the down main line. The works line became a loop from which a long siding ran southwards, parallel to the main line. At the end of the loop there were two sidings, one serving the newly-built large bank of kilns. The other siding led to the old kiln which may, thus, have still been in use at this time. By the end of the century the layout had been modified. Various later plans of the works show that the sidings were still approached by means of the trailing point from the main line, however the long siding had been removed. The original loop had now become two parallel loops. The locomotives of the North Eastern Railway (and later the London & North Eastern Railway) had right-of-way into the central road which was required to be kept empty of wagons as far as possible. The tracks from the end of the easterly loop and the central road, merged to serve the new kilns. The central road and the westerly loop then joined and a long curved siding extended for almost 200 yards into the quarry itself, thus facilitating the removal of wagons of 'raw' limestone and the bringing of coal. All of the sidings forming the standard gauge system were the property of Earl Grey who had paid for their initial installation. The sidings were normally shunted by the locomotive of a down goods train, that is, one heading towards Tweedmouth, any traffic for the south being remarshalled

LIME BURNERS.

Benson William & Son Ltd. Fourstones, Hexham
Richardson John, Little Mill quarries, Alnwick

LIME MERCHANTS.

Armstrong Rt. Railway st. Newcastle
Richardson John, Little Mill quarries, Alnwick

Kelly's Guide for 1938 recorded Richardson as one of just three Northumberland concerns associated with the lime industry.
Author's Collection

This is the site of' the 'coal depot' marked on the earlier plan where coal was transferred from wagons on the standard gauge siding, above the wall, into narrow gauge wagons waiting beneath. From here the coal was taken up an incline to charge the kilns. *Author*

Some sleepers from the narrow gauge railway survive, and are sometimes visible, beneath the surface of the water at this small pond below one of the former quarry faces near the entrance to the quarry. *Author*

there. When the later kiln was in use the long standard gauge siding was crossed by a bridge carrying the narrow gauge rails towards the kiln top.

In the early 1870s Alnwick Foundry is known to have supplied some 'carriages' and wheels to the works; their nature or function have not been discovered. Also, early in the Richardson era, the works were undergoing some ongoing modifications and improvements. The kilns were repaired in 1870 by a certain 'William Barker' (perhaps William Barkus from the Whinstone Quarry). This gentleman also built several retaining walls and some coal drops. Later the kilns were further relined using firebricks from the brickworks of the Radcliffe Coal Company at Amble in 1884. Yet more firebricks and fireclay were supplied by the Burradon and Coxlodge Coal Company in 1888. An auction sale, held around the same time, resulted in the works acquiring 20 wagons and 64 rail sleepers, followed later by another 13 wagons and 308 more sleepers. This is likely to have been for the construction of the 2 ft 6 in. narrow gauge system to link the quarry, the coal drops and the tops of the kilns.

An inventory (undated but certainly contemporary with the similar document for the whinstone quarry produced when Richardson took this over in the mid-1890s) indicates that the limestone quarry contained 25 waggons [*sic*], light rails from the quarry to the kiln bank, rails between the railway and the coal drops, seven points and four 'shifting ones' and 4,382 linear feet of railway rails. At this time horses were being used to move wagons around the site. In 1900 the works suffered its first fatality when a labourer, William Dawson, aged 24 was killed as he was shunting some wagons with a horse. In attempting to loosen a chain from one of the wagons whilst it was in motion he slipped, fell beneath the wagon, and was crushed to death. (This appears to have been the only railway accident at the quarry; however, a second fatality occurred in September 1913 when James Clark, another labourer, was crushed to death by a fall of surface clay when he was undercutting it, without taking any precautions.)

In 1907 Richardson was in touch with the W.G. Bagnall Locomotive Works in Stafford, and he obtained a copy of their catalogue listing 'Locomotives of all Descriptions, Light Railways, Turntables and Tipping Wagons.' It is not known whether Richardson ever obtained a locomotive from Bagnall's, however, a journal entitled *Machinery Market*, dated 26th September, 1924, contains an advertisement for a 2 ft 6 in. gauge locomotive to be sold at Little Mill. The locomotive was advertised as being built by Manning, Wardle (of Leeds). This locomotive may have been the first one to operate on the narrow gauge system at Little Mill.

Another locomotive obtained for the limestone quarry was obtained second-hand from Jee's Hartshill Granite & Brick Company, of Nuneaton in Warwickshire. It was an outside-cylindered saddle tank with the 0-4-0 wheel arrangement, originally built by the Hunslet Engine Company in Leeds in 1881, with works number HE 268/1881. This number was, in later years, confirmed from a stamp on the locomotive's motion. It also carried a plate reading 'James W. Ellis and Co. Ltd., Newcastle-on-Tyne. Rebuilt 1920 East Boldon'. The Industrial Railway Society records its arrival at Little Mill as being in 1907 via the Hunslet works. It was first owned by Drinkwater & Company in Dublin and carried the name *Fergus*. Later it worked for the Granite & Brick Company at Hartshill,

These are the remains of the powder store at Little Mill, apparently constructed from part of an old boiler. The remains are located a few yards to the west of the former coal depot and interchange sidings. *Author*

These impressive industrial archaeological remains form part of the abutments where a bridge (see the earlier plan) took the narrow gauge line to the kiln top over the standard gauge coal siding. Various sleepers survive in the ground on the top level. *Author*

This is a photograph, taken with permission in 2011, of the inside of the large kiln at Little Mill showing one of the draw holes from which the roasted lime would have been removed. Working inside a large kiln, such as this, would have been a hot and unpleasant occupation, highly injurious to good health. *Author*

This photograph of locomotive HE 268, built in 1881, is the only one so far discovered by the author, which shows it whilst it was still working at Little Mill, though in this picture it appears not to be 'in steam'. The picture was taken on 12th September, 1931. A pile of limestone lies in the foreground next to the locomotive. *Beamish Museum Collection*

This photograph of HE 268 was taken in 1947 close to the time of the cessation of quarrying at Little Mill. The locomotive had been out of use for some time when the photograph was taken. This photograph looks north. *Beamish Museum Collection*

Warwickshire. It had cylinders of 6 in. x 10 in. and wheels of 1 ft 8 in. diameter. It performed years of useful work at Little Mill until it was laid up around the time of World War II. After withdrawal from active service it remained in the quarry, mounted on a short length of rail, becoming more and more derelict. It was finally scrapped in about February 1951. Fortunately photographs of the locomotive survive, albeit mainly showing it in a derelict state.

The last known locomotive used at Little Mill was unique. In 1943, Richardson constructed, at Little Mill, a locomotive using a Hudson 4-wheeled wagon chassis. It was fitted with an Armstrong Siddeley car engine which was started using petrol but which then ran on paraffin. To provide extra weight to improve adhesion the wheels were filled with lead. Its axles were coupled by means of a chain and sprockets. The locomotive operated in the declining years of the quarry. After cessation of operations some parts of the locomotive were scrapped (1951) but the frame remained on site until about 1969 when it too was scrapped.

Fortunately several plans exist, dated 1896 and later, showing the extent of the narrow gauge rail system on which these locomotives and wagons ran. Unfortunately these plans are not of sufficient quality for reproduction here. That of 1896 shows a line running from the then-active quarry face on the south side of the quarry. It then split into two with one line heading towards the large kilns, the other towards the interchange sidings close to the 'coal wharf'. The single line leading towards the kilns then opened out to form a short loop, which later allowed the locomotive to run-round wagons that had been hauled from the quarry face. At the works end of the loop the line became single and climbed up the steep kiln bank before terminating on the top of the kilns. The line towards the coal drops formed a series of loops which ran parallel to the long standard gauge siding. Coal from the standard gauge wagons was discharged and loaded into the narrow gauge ones which were then propelled up to the top of the kilns, crossing over the standard gauge line. Charges of limestone and coal were added to the kilns, here, in a ratio of about 5:1. Later maps show that some alterations were made to the system, including simplification of the pattern of loops adjacent to the coal drops, and the lines in the quarry had been moved to where the active faces were located. In 1934 Richardson reported to the Howick Estates that the rails were in poor order.

After the closure of the quarry in the early 1950s it became a stackyard to house part of the country's 'strategic reserve of timber'; this was managed by Montague-Meyer Ltd on behalf of the Ministry of Works. The last of the timber was supposed to have been removed in 1959 but not all had been taken away by the end of that year. The nearby Littlemill [*sic*] passenger station, adjacent to the level crossing, had closed on 15th September, 1958.

Today the site of the former limeworks sidings can be seen to the south of the Little Mill level crossing, albeit heavily overgrown. A lane, signposted 'Limery', and located to the west of the level crossing leads to, and beyond, the former house of the Richardson family now known as 'The Limery'. This is in private ownership and the privacy of the owners should be respected. However, the lane passing this house is designated as a public footpath and it leads to a gate which permits entry to the former limestone quarry, now a nature reserve established by the Northumberland Wildlife Trust. It is known as the Evelyn

The first of these photographs of HE 268 is dated June 1947 whilst the second is undated but, judging by the growth of vegetation beside the track, comes from a later date. Both are taken looking southwards as the former 'coal depot' wall forms the background. The locomotive's works plate has been removed. Unlike the locomotive used in Richardson's whinstone quarry nearby this locomotive did not carry a name. *(Both) Beamish Museum Collection*

Howick Memorial (Littlemill) Nature Reserve. The information boards attached to the gate highlights the special nature of the quarry with its lime loving plants, such as fairy flax and the bulbous buttercup. It refers to the ponds and more waterlogged areas where coots, ducks and smooth newts live between the bulrushes. The reserve is often grazed by sheep. Beyond the furthest gate of the reserve it is possible to access the trackbed of the former lines leading to the more southerly and westerly faces of the quarry, parts of which are still exposed. The land is all part of the Howick Estates and permission should be sought to leave the path and wander around the kilns area.

On entering the reserve the kilns lie to the left of the trackway. The older, single-pot kiln is approachable along an incline though the kiln top is fenced off. Just to the east of this are the remains of the former bridge taking the narrow gauge tracks, leading to the top of the second six-pot kiln, over the standard gauge siding leading to the coal wharf. It is possible to gain access to the area next to the kiln top via an incline a little further to the east, though this involves ducking under the low branches of some small trees. At various points near the top of this incline are found decaying sleepers with bolts projecting vertically. There is also a large concrete structure, with projecting bolts, which is the likely remains of a World War II gun emplacement. Near the kiln top are several pieces of rail *in situ* including the 'frog' from some narrow gauge pointwork. The six pots of this large kiln are fenced off, preventing access, as their edges are crumbling. However, there is some good news. The Howick Estates have commenced (in June 2011) the external and internal restoration of the Grade II listed kiln buildings. The incline leading to the kilns from the quarry can be followed for a short distance to the site of the former bridge over the standard gauge siding. A panoramic view of the former quarry can be obtained from this point and the routes of the various branches to the different quarry faces are evident.

Retracing one's steps and crossing the nature reserve track allows access to a lower part of the quarry where part of the limestone quarry face is visible. This shows evidence of folding and faulting. Below the stone face is a small pond filling up the lowest levels. This is the breeding place and home of toads, newts and frogs. When the water level falls in summer it is sometimes possible to see a row of sleepers still *in situ*. Some 25 metres to the south lies the wharf where coal was transhipped from the standard gauge wagons into those of the narrow gauge system for transport to the kiln top. These are in a good state of preservation. Beyond this, at the side of the former trackbed can be seen the remains of the quarry's powder house built from an old boiler, surrounded by layers of stones. Aerial photographs of the area, available commercially on CD-ROM, also reveal the full extent of the site including the routes of the former sidings and the now-crumbling quarry faces.

It must be emphasized that the kilns, quarries and their surrounds are private property. In addition it is important to point out that the site is inherently dangerous with the currently crumbling kilns, the projecting sleepers and bits of trackwork, the steep and slippery slopes (especially after rain) and abrupt edges. Finally care should be taken not to disturb any sheep, or wildlife, in the quarry.

The unsuccessful efforts, in the late 1960s, to establish a narrow gauge railway preservation centre on this site were described in Volume One.

Above: Few of the quarry's wagons survived beyond World War II. This image, enlarged from a larger photograph, shows one wooden-bodied post-war survivor.

J.W. Armstrong Collection

Right: Some narrow-gauge rail remains, including a 'frog', several short lengths of rail, rusted track spikes and some heavily corroded sleepers, survive at the top of the embankment leading to the new kiln.

Author

To replace his worn out narrow gauge steam locomotive Richardson employed a home-made locomotive which consisted of an Armstrong Siddeley engine, driving, by means of a chain, a former wagon chassis. Eventually the engine was removed, but the chassis, shown from different angles in these two photographs taken in 1967, remained on site at Little Mill for some years before it was scrapped. *(Both) Dr C.G. Down*

The top of the new kiln provides an excellent vantage point from which to watch trains on the adjacent East Coast main line. Here a DRS-liveried class '47' is at the rear of a southward bound 'top-and-tailed' special train just south of Little Mill level crossing. Another class '47' was at the head of the train. *Author*

The sidings for Little Mill limeworks were located to the right of the East Coast main line taken from the nearby level crossing when it was safe to do so. Today the site is known as Little Mill Junction as there are crossovers between the up and down lines at this point. Both lines are signalled for bi-directional running. The whinstone sidings were on the left. *Author*

12 - The Longhoughton and Ratcheugh Quarry Railways

The linked Longhoughton and Ratcheugh Quarries (centred on NU235156 and NU230152 respectively) lie at the side of the road leading from Denwick to Longhoughton. They are located about three miles east-north-east of Alnwick.

Longhoughton Quarry is aligned in an approximately north-easterly direction from the entrance gate by the road. Staring in the second half of the 19th century it was first quarried for limestone. Later it became a whinstone quarry, the latter being of much greater economic importance. This quarry is no longer worked. The adjacent Ratcheugh Quarry, to the left of the main entrance gate, has always been purely for extraction of whinstone and is still being worked intermittently.

A very small quarry, at the point where Ratcheugh and Longhoughton quarries meet, is recorded on the first Ordnance Survey maps in the 1860s. This quarry must have been developed after about 1830 because there is no trace of the quarry on Greenwoods map of 1827 or other plans dating from this time. By the publication date of the OS maps of the 1890s this 'Longhoughton Quarry' had been considerably extended. By the early 1920s Longhoughton had been extended both north-eastwards and eastwards, with stone being removed from two levels, though the stone being extracted at this time was largely whinstone. In 1922 it is recorded that just two workers were employed in the quarrying of limestone at Longhoughton but 49 were involved in the removal of whinstone at the newly developing Ratcheugh Quarry nearby.

As mentioned in Volume Three which dealt with whinstone quarrying, the first concern, involved with the stone industry in the locality, was the Northumberland Whinstone Co. Ltd which was quarrying stone at Longhoughton by 1887. (It was the Northumberland Whinstone Quarry which, much later, introduced a locomotive-hauled tramway system into Longhoughton and Ratcheugh quarries. However, maps depict this as serving the whinstone quarry faces and it has not been possible to discover if the limestone faces were similarly served.)

After removal from the stone faces and crushing the limestone was taken from the quarries by horse-drawn carts. There was no kiln on site so it was always 'raw' limestone that was led away. Some was delivered directly to local destinations though other stone was carted to the nearby Longhoughton Sidings where it was loaded into wagons for onward movement by rail. The total of 30,000 tons of stone removed from Longhoughton sidings in 1913 did not separately indicate the quantity of limestone.

A second concern to have operated at Longhoughton in the early years of the 20th century was H.G. Prowde Ltd, often referred to at Longhoughton and elsewhere as 'McLaren and Prowde'. Prowde's quarry was adjacent to that of the Northumberland Whinstone Co. and was, somewhat confusingly, also named Longhoughton Quarry. Prowde's lease was for the quarrying of both limestone and whinstone, but there is no evidence that this concern ever operated a tramway or railway within this quarry despite the 'standard' terms of the Lease which permitted the firm to do so.

Although both cartographic evidence, and the evidence provided by surviving quarrymen, can provide details of the extent and workings of the later Longhoughton and Ratcheugh whinstone quarry lines, together with their wagons and locomotives, there is no-one alive today who has memories of the quarrying of limestone there. No documentary evidence of the use of railways associated with the limestone industry at this site has been discovered. However, a now-deceased quarryman who lived locally and worked, from the 1920s onwards, at the Craster and nearby Howick Quarries, recalled a pile of old, worn, rails lying in Longhoughton Quarry when he made a visit in the very early years of locomotive-hauled trains on the whinstone tramway system. These may have been from an earlier use of rails to transport quarried limestone from the quarry face.

A description of the present-day Longhoughton Quarry appeared in the Volume Three in this series. It is mainly visited by anglers, bird watchers and those exercising their dogs. It also receives parties of student geologists as the quarry is now designated as being an SSSI. It contains some bands of marble, formed when hot molten material (which formed whinstone on cooling and solidifying), came into contact with limestone, resulting in its metamorphosis.

Longhoughton Quarry, which provided both limestone and whinstone, has now become a recreational area used by fishermen, dog walkers and birdwatchers. The nearby Ratcheugh Quarry has recently reopened (late 2011) supplying whinstone. *Author*

Chapter Seven

The Tramways at Pauperhaugh and Ward's Hill Quarries

These two limestone quarries are located to the south-east of Rothbury. For neither of them is the evidence of tramways conclusive. However, a combination of 'suggestions' from cartographic evidence, from oral evidence and on site investigations permits their inclusion here. Both were small concerns, dating from Victorian times, and were operated by just a small labour force. Local archives contain no documents relating to the workings of either of the quarries and it is unlikely that any documentary evidence of the quarries' operations has survived, unless it resides in private hands.

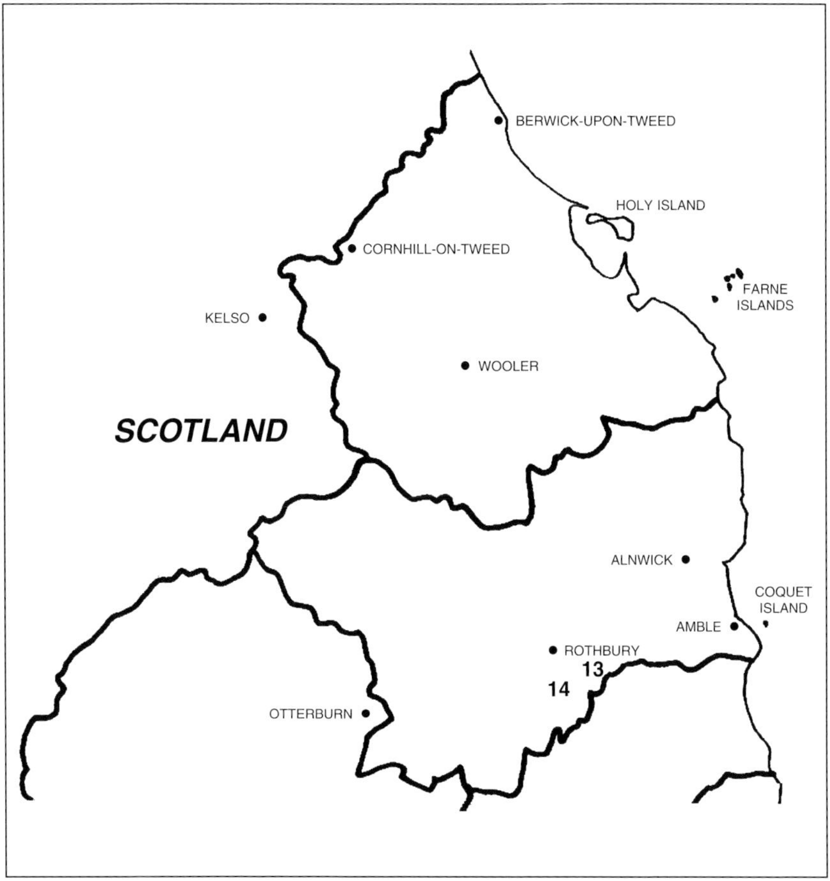

Pauperhaugh quarry is not especially photogenic as much has been filled in with rubble and covered with topsoil on which shrubs and bushes are starting to grow tall. The mound on which the kiln was located was recorded in a late 20th century survey and is still just identifiable at the north end of the quarry. *Author*

The limestone quarry at Ward's Hill is located adjacent to the road and there are no roadside fences. Some of the vertical stone faces are visible but much of the quarry is now covered with grass which is grazed by livestock. *Author*

13 - The Pauperhaugh Quarry and Limeworks Tramway

The Pauperhaugh or Brinkburn limestone quarry (NZ 110996) was located to the east side of the road linking Longframlington and Pauperhaugh, some 200 yards to the north of the farm at Brinkburn New Houses. It is shown as a working quarry in the first edition Ordnance Survey maps published in the 1860s. The kiln was located towards the north side of the quarry and a cart- or trackway linked the base of the kiln with the nearby road. The source of coal for the kiln was possibly the coal shaft at New Houses, but there was also a small coal pit marked on the same map to the north of the quarry. In subsequent map editions the features are marked as 'Old Quarry' and 'Old limekiln' indicating their closure.

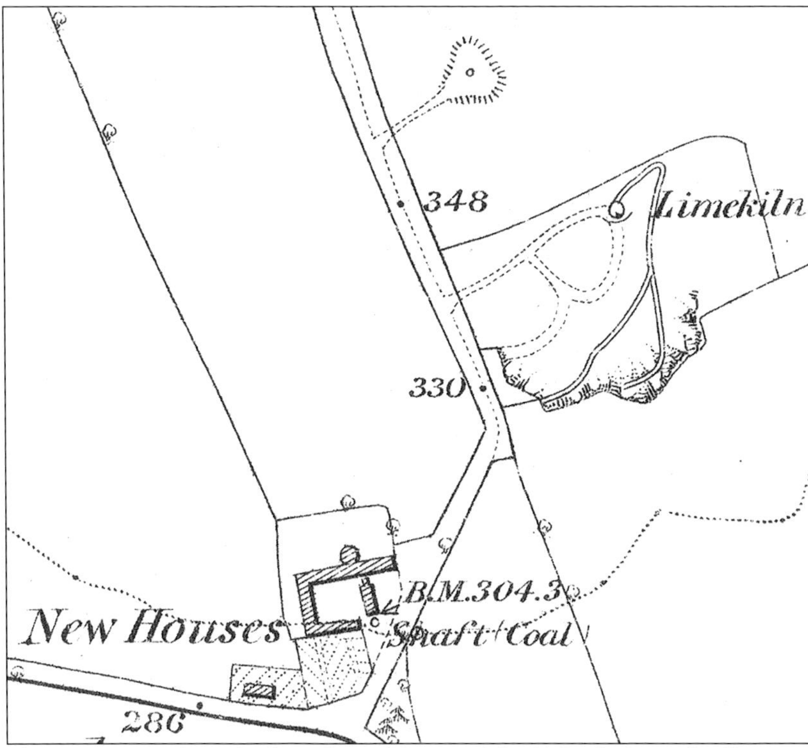

This is an extract from the first edition OS map of the 1860s. It shows that limestone quarry was located to the east of the minor road linking Pauperhaugh with Longframlington. The kiln was located in the north-east corner of the quarry. The track to the kiln top is recorded on the map in the same way as the Brinkburn Wagonway located a few hundred yards away to the west. Across the road from the quarry was a small mine which probably supplied the coal for roasting the lime. Its shaft was filled in or capped some time ago, for part of the yard of Brinkburn New Houses Farm now occupies its site.
Ordnance Survey, Crown Copyright, All Rights Reserved

It has been suggested, locally, that to link the quarry face on the south side of the quarry with the top of the kiln there was a small tramway. The surveyor's and cartographer's distinction, on the 1860s map, between the cartway or cart-track leading to the road, and the route leading to the top of the kilns, suggests that the latter may well have been a small tramway, probably of narrow gauge and hand- or horse-worked. It is certainly recorded on the map in the same manner as the nearby Brinkburn Wagonway (*see the map in Volume Two*). In view of the gradient from the quarry faces to the top of the kilns it is likely that horses were used to haul the wagons. In the mid-19th century a smithy was built in the hamlet of Pauperhaugh nearby. The ironworks, the limestone quarry, the coal and iron pits and the nearby farms would, no doubt, have been the smith's customers.

The lime from the quarry was probably used locally for agricultural purposes though the nearby Brinkburn ironworks may have used some of the limestone as a flux. Unfortunately no documentary evidence appears to have survived which could confirm this or identify the quarry and kiln operators.

The quarry received an archaeological survey in the 1970s when the survival of the base of the old kiln was recorded. No reference was made in the survey report relating to a possible tramway, though the alignment, marked on the map, had already been hidden below several metres of tipped materials. Today the quarry, located on private land, has been largely filled in and covered with a layer of topsoil, but it can be approached, with permission, from a gate at the roadside. However, there is very little of interest for the visitor to see.

14 - The Ward's Hill Limestone Quarry Tramway

Ward's Hill is found about two miles south-west of Pauperhaugh bridge (near the B6334, Rothbury to Weldon Bridge road) and half a mile east of the B6342 at Forestburn Gate.

In the mid-19th century a large kiln was built just to the north-east of the present Wardshill Wood by the side of what became a limestone quarry of several acres (NZ072966). Local coal was used to roast the lime; the ordnance map of the mid-1890s shows an 'Old coal shaft' immediately adjacent to the quarry. The operator at this time was believed to have been a certain Mr Brown though nothing more seems to be known about him. By the early years of the 20th century the undertaking was operated, according to local resident Stan Shotton, by Messrs T. & C. Proudlock who lived at nearby Pauperhaugh. Apparently a short narrow gauge tramway line was laid to move the limestone from the quarry faces to the kiln. The line formed a curved route, its tubs serving various faces in the quarry, before being hauled up a slope and arriving at the top of the kiln. Horses were used to haul the tubs.

This was a landsale quarry, the lime being sold to anyone who turned up with a cart or even a basket. The lime was used principally on the land, though some slaked lime was used as a 'wash' for the outside of buildings. The quarries, in the ownership of Rothbury Rural District Council by the 1920s, continued to supply lime on a very small scale until just before World War II.

In 1922, for example, just two men are recorded as being employed at the quarry. Since World War II Ordnance Survey maps have marked the quarries as 'disused'. The 'old kiln' is marked on maps up to the present day, though no tramway has ever been indicated on OS maps. The apparent absence of any other documentation makes a more detailed description of the quarry and its tramway impossible.

The quarry and kiln lie on unfenced land at the side of the road which crosses Ward's Hill to the south of the former colliery at The Lee. With care their remains can be inspected on foot, though some steep and crumbling rock faces, and (especially in winter) some slippery paths and standing water, make visits to some parts hazardous. Sheep are often found grazing in the quarry. Parking for a vehicle is easy at the side of the Ward's Hill road by the quarry, though local cattle can show an interest in parked vehicles, damage having been caused to wing mirrors. Cattle grids on the road restrict the wanderings of the livestock.

The former limekiln at Ward's Hill is now in derelict condition and subject to erosion from the action of frost and rain. It can be inspected though care is essential as some of the kiln's stone is crumbling away. This photograph was taken in 2010. *Author*

The standard gauge branch of the Greenleighton Coal & Lime Co. branched off to the right, towards the limeworks at Rothley Shield, just beyond the road bridge seen at the west end of Longwitton station on the North British Railway's Rothbury branch. Note the old coach body on the platform. *'Photos from the Fifties'*

A storm is brewing in the background as the local farmer collects some stone from Greenleighton Quarry to fill in a hole in his farm drive. At the time of writing it is some 30 years since the last limestone, for Kielder Reservoir works, was quarried at Greenleighton. *Author*

Chapter Eight

The Limestone Railways of Greenleighton, Hartington and Ritton White House

These quarries are located about 15 miles south-west of Alnwick and are best approached from the Rothbury to Hexham road, now the B6342.

A casual visitor to this area at the start of the 21st century would be forgiven for believing that this area had always been a rural backwater, yet it formerly possessed several small coal pits, then a colliery, quarries and a large limeworks. Later still, in the 20th century, there was even an opencast pit here.

Both small-scale coal mining, in several small pits at Longwitton, and limestone quarrying at quarries at Greenleighton and Hartington, had taken place in the first half of the 19th century but it was not until the coming of the North British Railway's Scots Gap to Rothbury branch that the scale of local industry increased. The story of this branch railway line is told by Stanley Jenkins in his book *The Rothbury Branch* published by the Oakwood Press.

This view of the cutting leading from Greenleighton Quarry, taken in 1967 shortly after track-lifting, can be contrasted with the view below taken from the same position in 2010. In the intervening time the trees have grown considerably and the building has been demolished.
Dr C.G. Down

Although W.T. Bathgate's 20th century line from Greenleighton was only of narrow gauge, the same exit from the quarry was used by the standard gauge line of the Greenleighton Coal & Lime Co. until 1885; hence the wide cutting and trackbed at this point. *Author*

In the mid-19th century Sir Walter Trevelyan owned the whole of the local Estate. A private halt, initially known as 'Rothley' was constructed on the newly-opened NBR Rothbury branch but in 1873 it became a public station. Its name was changed to 'Longwitton'. It was located just over 3¼ miles from Scots Gap. It was to the west of this station that a standard gauge line was constructed to serve the lime industries which were to develop just a few years later based on Greenleighton Quarry.

In August 1874 a Lease was drawn up between the Wallington Estate and a consortium known as the Longwitton and Greenleighton Coal & Lime Co. The composition of this consortium was described in Volume Two dealing specifically with the Longwitton Colliery and its railway. This consortium planned to produce coal, limestone, common bricks, tiles, and firebricks. They planned that half of the output from their Longwitton Colliery would be needed to fire the Greenleighton kilns. The lease was to take effect from October 1874 and was planned to last for a period of 20 years. It permitted the company to lease about 100 acres of land and to build limekilns, railways and tramways. The railways were to be built from the Rothbury branch to both the colliery and kilns involving the laying of nearly two miles of rail of 'full gauge'. The lease involved the payment of £200 per annum increasing in stages to £250 then £300 as output increased. In addition there was to be a payment of 9*d*. per ton of lime removed and £20 annually for the use of the limekilns. They expected to employ 100 men and produce 900 tons of lime per week!

15 - W.T. Bathgate (Lime Works) Ltd

'Bathgates', a Scottish firm from Midlothian, arrived on the scene in 1938. Mr W.T. ('Willy') Bathgate had looked at several nearby sites, including Cartington and Tosson, with a view to the establishment of a limeworks locally. Having inspected Greenleighton Quarry and kilns he established a presence there, trading under the name of W.T. Bathgate (Limeworks) Ltd. Bathgate's company was actually incorporated on 2nd January, 1941 with the registration number SC 021641.

He quickly reopened the quarry (NZ034917) to the north of that used by the Longwitton company and built a ¼ mile-long narrow gauge railway between this quarry and the 1870s kilns which he refurbished and reopened. The entrance to the quarry was at a height of about 820 ft, with the line descending to the kilns at about 785 ft. Bathgates did not contemplate rebuilding the line as far as the Rothbury branch (though this was still open). Instead the products of his quarry and kilns would be distributed by road, the local roads having by that date been well surfaced by the county council. Various local hauliers were involved and the lime was distributed throughout Northumberland and into the Scottish Borders, for example to Duns and Kelso. Some 'kibbled lime' (finely crushed but unroasted limestone) was used by local farmers. Only occasional sheeted wagons of lime were dispatched from Longwitton station.

Bathgate's railway was a 2 ft gauge line and it employed small 4-wheeled diesel-mechanical locomotives built by Ruston & Hornsby Ltd of Lincoln. The

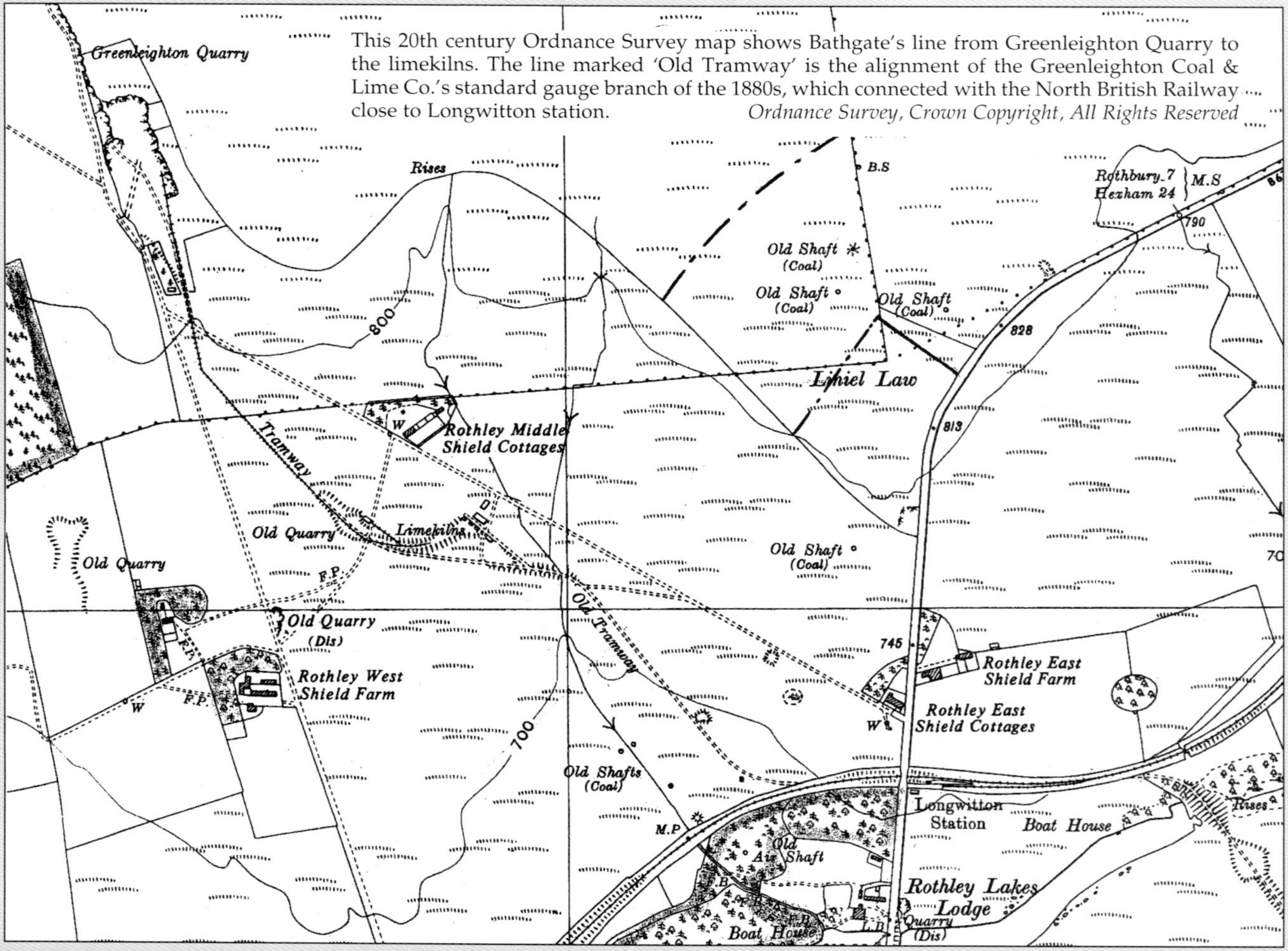

This 20th century Ordnance Survey map shows Bathgate's line from Greenleighton Quarry to the limekilns. The line marked 'Old Tramway' is the alignment of the Greenleighton Coal & Lime Co.'s standard gauge branch of the 1880s, which connected with the North British Railway close to Longwitton station. *Ordnance Survey, Crown Copyright, All Rights Reserved*

lightweight track was spiked to wooden sleepers and some crushed limestone formed a thin layer of ballast. Various points and moveable sidings served the stone faces in the quarry, some of which rose to a height of 40 ft. The 'main' line left the quarry at its south end, passing some of the quarry buildings. These buildings included a low brick building with a corrugated iron roof which housed the workmen's bothy, the generator and the store. There was a separate explosives store, well away from the quarry faces, where the black powder, used for blasting, was kept. There was also a building to house the compressor for the operation of the drills. After a short cutting the railway crossed over the road leading to Greenleighton and Dyke Head farms, and curved, in a slight cutting, towards the south-east. As the line approached the kilns it passed the blacksmith's workshop and climbed a substantial embankment. To the left was a siding, trailing in from the engine shed, where the locomotives were serviced and kept overnight. (The tank to hold the diesel fuel was not located at the shed. Instead it was located on stone pillars at the quarry entrance.)At the top of the kilns were two wagon turntables allowing the contents of the V-shaped hopper wagons to be tipped into any of the three pots. Generally two out of the three were in use at any one time. There were other buildings located by the kilns including a hydrating plant for slaking the roasted lime. The coal for roasting the lime was obtained from elsewhere, the sources including, in later years, Bathgate's own drift mines at Ward's Hill, a few miles away in the Rothbury direction, close to his Whinstone Quarry.

At the start of World War II just one locomotive, RH195844, obtained new from Ruston's in 1939, proved to be sufficient for the operation of the rail system. Wartime brought several problems, one being the need to shield the otherwise open tops of the fired kilns to make them less visible to enemy aircraft. Bathgate's obtained several other Ruston locomotives to cope with the increased business after the war finished. Four were obtained new from Ruston's (Works Nos. RH195844/1939, RH229654/1945, 235653/1946 and 252853/1947). Two were also obtained second-hand, these being RH211667/1941 which arrived from Cohen Ltd, of Hebburn Yard, Jarrow, and RH223716/1944, the last to arrive, which came from the Thornton Engineering Co. Ltd, of Whitley Bay in 1960, having worked earlier at Fence Houses Brickworks Ltd, in County Durham. When, in the early 1960s, Willy Bathgate opened his whinstone quarry at Ward's Hill (q.v.) he was able to transfer two of these locomotives to that site, for only two locomotives were generally used at a time at Greenleighton, one serving the tracks to the faces in the quarry and one working on the 'main' line. The others were either under repair or kept as spare locomotives in working order. Of the two locomotives transferred to Ward's Hill RH195844 was ultimately returned to Greenleighton whilst RH235653 remained there.

When Chris Down visited Greenleighton in August 1967 he noted that the rail system was partly complete but out of use. His sketch map of the quarry shows a loop and a shortened siding. Halfway along the line he recorded RH195844 inside the engine shed together with another locomotive which he could not identify. Off the rails, was the 20DL RH229654. This last locomotive had been fitted with a seat, which he presumed to have been removed from a tractor; it bore the legend 'Cammo Foundry'. There was no evidence of the other

Willy Bathgate's limekilns at Greenleighton appear not to have been working when this photograph was taken in the winter of 1955. The roasted lime was taken away by means of the road leading away from the photographer. This connected with the Rothbury to Scots Gap road near to Longwitton station. *The late Jack Hall's Collection*

This picture, taken some 10 years later from almost the same vantage point, shows the lime works shortly after cessation of lime burning. Several wagons are at the kiln top and the office, mess room and plant are still intact. *Dr C.G. Down*

Not many photographers ventured onto a kiln top to take photographs when a kiln was fired. However, here the photographer recorded three of Bathgate's workers loading lime into one of the pots. Some one cwt side-tipping wagons appear on the right-hand side of the picture.

The late Jack Hall's Collection

The entire complement of workers at Greenleighton limeworks enjoys a break outside the mess room at Greenleighton sometime in 1948. Willy Bathgate is seated third from the left on the back row, leaning against the mess room door. *Thompson Bathgate Collection*

W.T. 'Willy' Bathgate was one of six brothers who all worked in the lime industry. They are all pictured here in a 'family line-up' at a limeworks in Scotland. Willy is the shortest of the six, the fourth from the left-hand side. A loaded tub is partly hidden behind the brothers on the left.

Thompson Bathgate Collection

A Leyland 350 'Super Comet' lorry is loaded with lime at Rothley Shield limeworks, Greenleighton. In the foreground one of the Seddon lorries belonging to the haulier Telfer, of Scots Gap, awaits its turn for loading. This photograph, showing a side-tipping wagon on top of the kiln, was taken in 1965, just two years before the closure of the works. *The late Jack Hall's Collection*

locomotives which had worked here. (On the same day he visited Ward's Hill Quarry where he found the frame of the former Greenleighton locomotive RH235653 dumped on the incline leading from the quarry. The engine itself, with its bonnet and bulkheads, was being used to power a mobile screen. Some of Bathgate's Hudson-built 'Rugga' skips were on site, looking 'old'.)

The last Greenleighton locomotives were scrapped by the end of December 1967. The remaining track was lifted and disposed of by February 1968.

Bathgate finally sold his Greenleighton quarry as a going concern to Slater & Co. of Pickering, North Yorkshire, who operated the quarry for between two and three years. They used a portable crusher in the quarry for crushing the limestone which was taken away by road.

Willy Bathgate had also operated Middleton Lime Works at Gorebridge, Midlothian (managed by a certain R.H. Bathgate, presumably a relative). However, the *Edinburgh Gazette* of 1st April, 1986 contained a statement that Murdoch L. McKillop of Charlotte Square, Edinburgh had been appointed as Receiver of the assets of Bathgate's company. It was restored to the Register of Companies in January 1990 but is now recorded as 'Dissolved'. At present Middleton lime works is owned by a certain James Reid & Co. selling 'Dimension Stone'.

An attempt was made to demolish the kilns, for safety reasons, in 1969. This proved to be a difficult task in view of their size and the nature of their construction. Eventually explosives were used to break up the upper portion and this was followed by bulldozing of the debris. The lower portion was finally buried under a landscaped mound. The engine shed, hydrating plant and blacksmith's shop were demolished at the same time.

Jack Hall was the driver of this Seddon vehicle of J.R.M. Telfer which is recorded delivering some Greenleighton agricultural lime to a farmer at Denholm, near Hawick, in Scotland, in the mid-1960s. *The late Jack Hall Collection*

These two photographs, taken on 29th August 1967, show the interior of Greenleighton Quarry shortly after the closure of Bathgate's lime works. The first shows the hopper used for loading limestone into the tipper wagons which were usually operated in 'rakes' of five. The second photograph shows the line of narrow gauge rails leading from the hopper towards the quarry entrance. A run-round loop exists in the middle distance and, close to this, there was formerly a siding for storage of empty wagons. *(Both) Dr C.G. Down*

This photograph shows Bathgate's locomotive shed a short distance from the lime kilns. On the left inside the shed door was a single line of rails, the area to the right being used as a workshop and repair area. The quarry entrance is by the trees to the extreme right whilst the running line is on the embankment to the left. *Dr C.G. Down*

A glimpse of part of Bathgate's loco RH 195844 is seen on the rails on the left-hand side in the foreground, with a small part of RH 229564 being visible, off the rails, on the right. The photographer did not record the identity of the locomotive in the centre but it may well be RH 211667 which was one of the last two surviving locos at this site. Note the home-made weather boards on this locomotive! *Dr C.G. Down*

At the kiln top are several of the tipper wagons used to transport limestone from the quarry. On the extreme right is the top of the hydration plant whilst on the left, beyond a pile of lime, is the tiny cabin, or bothy, used by the workmen for shelter in extreme weather conditions.
Dr C.G. Down

A line of tipper wagons rests at the kiln top adjacent to the workmen's cabin. Five wagons was the normal size of 'a rake' at this works. A pile of lime is stacked on the left-hand side in this view which points towards the north-east. *Dr C.G. Down*

Quantities of limestone were removed from the quarry by road in subsequent years, the last being in 1982. For example some Greenleighton limestone was used in the construction of the Kielder dam and reservoir in the late 1970s and early 1980s. The *Greenleighton Moor Walk* booklet, published by the National Trust, refers to some two million tons of stone having been removed from the quarry in total! It is now protected as an SSSI on account of the rich fossil marine fauna within its rocks. Also the quarry faces are occasionally used by rock-climbers. Open cast mining has removed much of the traces of the former railway between the kilns and the Rothbury branch.

Today the quarry face can be viewed from the nearby public roadway where there is limited parking for cars, and part of the route of the former narrow gauge line, part in cutting, some on a shallow embankment, can be followed as far as the kilns. The open cast mining has removed the alignment of the former standard gauge 'mineral line' linking the former Rothbury branch and the kilns. The site of the former sidings and Longwitton station can be viewed from the road overbridge.

16 - The Hartington Tramways

One, perhaps two, 19th century tramways were located at Hartington, one being linked to the Rothbury branch of the North British Railway, the other being a possible line within the confines of a limestone quarry and by its associated limeworks. The first of these is the Hartington Quarry Tramway.

A small quarry was located in a field, known as 'Little Close' (NZ029883), belonging to Tuthill Farm at Hartington. It was linked by a short tramway, possibly of standard gauge, with the NBR's Rothbury branch between Scots Gap and Longwitton stations. The quarry, known as Hartington Quarry, is not shown as being in existence at the time of the first Ordnance Survey but is marked as an 'Old Quarry' by the time of second survey in the 1890s. The trackbed of the line is marked on the same maps as 'Old Tramway'. It was thus short-lived. The field containing the quarry shows evidence of 'rigg and furrow' agricultural use from earlier times.

Various suggestions have been put forward for the function of the quarry and its tramway. Firstly it has been suggested that stone from the quarry was used by the North British Railway, or a contractor, for or during the construction of the nearby Hartington Lane road underbridge. Secondly, investigations have shown that within the gaps in the whinstone in the quarry there are calcite veins (a crystalline form of calcium carbonate) with a high concentration of lead; it has been suggested that the line was built for the exploitation of this mineral, to be taken away via NBR metals. It is a local tradition to relate the legend that a local man, who was killed in the serious railway accident at nearby Donkin Rigg, had invested in, and profited from, this mineral venture and thus finally lost his life very close to the place where he had made his money. In this 1875 NBR accident four persons died, including one later in hospital, and 25 were injured. It occurred when six passenger vehicles, eight stone wagons and a couple of brake vans fell down an embankment. The branch is on a gradient of 1 in 75 at this point. The

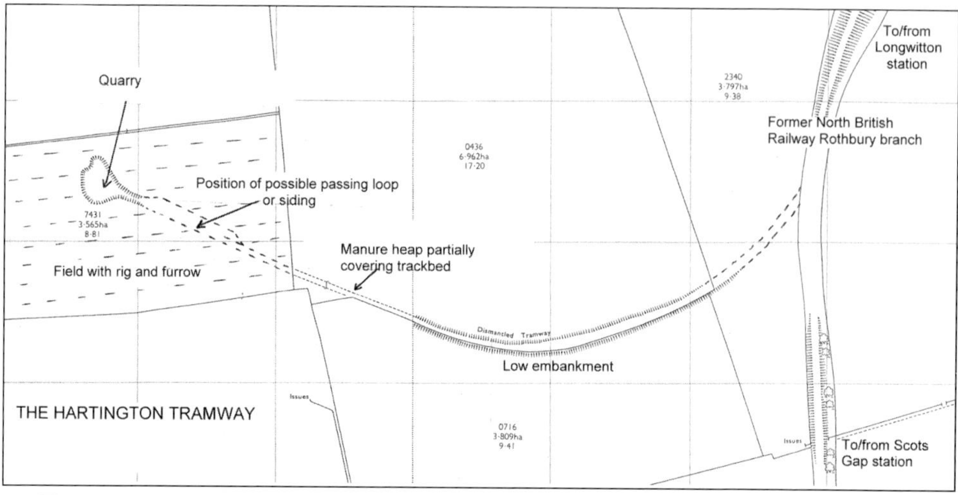

The Hartington Tramway, whose function is still unconfirmed, left the North British Railway's Rothbury branch between Scots Gap and Longwitton stations. The 'possible passing loop' was perhaps possibly used for storing empty wagons awaiting filling at the quarry, or for 'fulls' awaiting collection. *Ordnance Survey, Crown Copyright, All Rights Reserved*
By Permission Harry Beamish, National Trust

This photograph shows the easterly quarry face at Hartington Hill Quarry. An archaeological survey suggested the use of a small tramway here for moving the quarry's products. An inclined plane leads in the direction of the kilns. *Author*

dead included the train's guard and a pattern maker. The other two dead were a mason and a contractor with, perhaps, the credentials to have been the gentleman associated with the quarry, always assuming the legend contains some truth.

Most of the tramway lies on private land and permission must be sought from the local farm to walk over it. The quarry contains some dumped materials and its edges are somewhat eroded but the route of the line can be followed easily as far as the junction with the branch. The quarry itself is very wet, a seasonal spring emerging at the site. The trackbed descends a fairly steep gradient from the quarry, the contours marked on OS maps indicating that the junction is some 80 ft below the land level at the quarry. As a result of the 'sideways slope' of the land, some earthworks were needed during the construction of the tramway line and these low embankments have survived as the fields have been used for stock rearing rather than being ploughed for arable purposes. A modern fence follows the side of the tramway for part of its length. In two locations it appears that the trackbed was wide enough to accommodate more than one line of rails: close to the quarry and adjacent to the junction with the NBR line. These may have been for wagon storage or as passing loops. No evidence of old rails, either *in situ* or as fence posts has been discovered. Nothing is known of how the tramway was operated, though it is likely that horses were used as the motive power.

The second tramway at Hartington is the likely Hartington Hill Limestone Tramway which is believed to have served Hartington Hill quarry and limeworks. References to this line appear in an archaeological survey report for the site.

The Hartington Hill quarry (NZ024888) and limeworks were located on the south side of Gallows Hill north of High Hartington, just a few hundred yards to the north-east of the quarry line previously described. They were still in use in the 1860s. Labourers, listed in the 1871 census and domiciled at Hartington, may well have worked there. By the 1890s the quarries were described on Ordnance Survey maps as 'Disused'. The first edition OS maps identify trackways in, and near, the quarry which are likely to have been the alignments of tramways, as they show, for example, what appear to be sidings leading to the quarry faces and a route to the top of the kilns. However, no documentary evidence relating to the operation of the kilns or the tramways has so far been discovered.

The two-pot kiln, built from local sandstone, survives today in a good state of preservation. and is an impressive structure. It lies on private land, sometimes grazed by livestock. Fortunately a public footpath starting at the side of High Hartington Cottages leads past the site and it is possible to inspect the kiln and quarries from this. Various weathered gradients leading towards the kilns from the quarry may have been the tramway alignments though the final part of the gradient to the top of the kilns is very steep indeed. It is likely that the lines were of narrow gauge. Stables at one of the nearby farms could have provided the horse power. Alternatively various local carters would have used their own horses either to operate in the quarry or to haul away the roasted lime, believed to have been used mainly for agricultural purposes. An old trackway, now grass-covered, leads down the hillside from the base of the kilns. There was never a connection to the nearby NBR line.

In the spring of 2007 repairs were started to the stonework of the kilns. These are now complete. Now registered as a listed building and under the protection of the National Trust, the future of the kilns is thus secure.

The embankment of the Hartington Tramway can be seen beyond the second field in this picture taken from the footpath which now occupies the trackbed of the former Rothbury branch.
Author

This is the first view of the Hartington Kiln kilns that you get from the track leading up from High Hartington Cottages and the farm at Tuthill. The kilns are now listed buildings and have recently received comprehensive repairs. The quarry lies hidden, directly behind the kilns.
Author

Further details of the tramway would probably require excavations at the site, alternatively the discovery of some documentation dating from the time of the quarry's operation.

The draw holes for removing the roasted lime are visible in this view of the 'interior' of the kilns at Hartington Hill. This lime is believed to have been used for local agricultural purposes. *Author*

Ritton White House Quarry is seen on the right-hand side of this present-day photograph. The house, after which the quarry and tramway were named, is the tallest of the buildings in the centre of the picture. The tramway descended the hillside from the quarry entrance. *Author*

The embankment of the former Ritton Whitehouse Tramway, descending towards the kilns of the 'Ritton Whitehouse Lime Works', stands out in this 'across-the-fields' photograph taken from the track which leads to the Fontburn Reservoir. *Author*

17 - The Ritton Whitehouse Limestone Tramway

The limestone quarry, very near to Ritton Whitehouse (alternatively Ritton White House: NZ056945), was in operation, on a small scale, from about 1860. A mile to the east at Ritton Colt Park new farms were being developed. The lime from this first quarry very close to Ritton White House was used to improve the soil quality on these farms, the land having formerly been moorland of an acid nature. It is not known who operated the quarry at this time

By 1870 it is known that Francis and William Armstrong were quarrying lime at Ritton White House and were operating a lime kiln. It was at about this time that limestone quarrying moved from the first quarry, close to Ritton White House, to a second which was located some 400 yards to the south (NZ056941).

A narrow gauge tramway was constructed to facilitate the movement of limestone, both to the kilns (at what became known as 'Ritton White House Limeworks'), and to a siding off the North British Railway's Rothbury branch, for transhipment of limestone rubble. Many wagons of rubble from the quarry loaded at this siding were taken the short journey along what were presumably contractor's tracks to form the embankment approaches to Fontburn viaduct on the Rothbury branch which was being built nearby.

The first kiln at the limeworks was located at NZ051943. In 1883 a second kiln was constructed and in the following year (on 29th November) a permanent siding, referred to above, was opened to link the limeworks to the completed NBR line. The quarry tramway, partly on an embankment to even out the gradient, was just over 500 yards in length and horses provided the motive power. It ran almost due east-west from the quarry exit to the kiln top. Shortly after the line left the quarry a short tramway branch trailed in from the south. It linked with a much smaller quarry lower down the hillside. This was only some 50 yards in length. There was a downhill gradient from the main quarry to the kilns and sidings, thus facilitating the movement of the loaded narrow gauge wagons. At the lower end of the line one tramway siding served the tops of the kilns whilst another served what was known as the 'raw stone dock', that is, the transhipment siding for rubble. A second standard gauge siding was later laid to this stone dock. A short 'headshunt' siding was located where the sidings joined the Rothbury branch; coal from the nearby Whitehouse Colliery was transhipped at this point. It is recorded that horses were used to remove the wagons left by the NBR branch goods trains and place them into the appropriate place in the sidings. The sidings were about 250 yards in length and, at first, and for some years, lacked a loop for 'runround' purposes. Early in the history of the Rothbury branch these sidings came under the auspices of Longwitton station, a ground frame being located in a small hut opposite the railway cottages at the sidings. Later Ewesley became the block post and control of all of the sidings near White House (i.e. those for the limeworks, Font Siding and Fontburn Goods) passed to that station. These later additions to the siding network were as a result of the construction of the Fontburn reservoir (q.v.) and the small passenger station.

The precise date of transfer of the limeworks and tramway from the Armstrongs to the Ewesley Quarry Co. Ltd has not been discovered. However, it was this latter company which was leasing the works from the Ordes, the local landowners, by the early 1900s. The Ewesley Quarry Company's registered office was situated at Guildhall Chambers, Sandhill, in Newcastle.

In 1902 a small station halt, called 'Whitehouse' was built on the Rothbury branch close to the limeworks sidings. It cost the princely sum of £185 and had a small waiting shed and booking office. To avoid confusion between this station and Whitehouse in Aberdeenshire it was renamed 'Fontburn' on 1st May, 1904. The Whitehouse sidings are recorded as being temporarily closed in 1904 but some stone and lime may well have been supplied for the construction of the Fontburn dam in the years preceding this. Certainly, after the temporary period of closure, the Ewesley company continued to operate the quarry, tramway and kilns up to 1914. There was then a further period of closure before they reopened briefly in the early 1920s. The products may have been taken away by road at this time. In the meantime the station at Fontburn had been closed to passengers (3rd October, 1921) but it was immediately reopened as a halt, with its nameboard being changed to read 'Fontburn Halt'.

Fortunately a map, drawn up for the LNER shortly after the 'Grouping' in the early 1920s, records the maximum extent of the railway system at the sidings. A loop had been provided on the Rothbury branch opposite Fontburn station. A short headshunt existed at the Ewesley end of this loop. The loop ended opposite the railway workmen's cottages (later 'Daisy Cottages'). From the loop two parallel sidings led towards the limeworks, now being connected by a crossover to form a loop. The LNER property ended at the works end of the right-hand siding and at the branch end of the other. Beyond the end of the sidings loop, the line split into two lines of rail leading towards the kilns, one still acting as the transhipment siding. (By this time the Ewesley Quarry Co. were starting to extract igneous stone from their new quarry to the east and a line led from the 'limeworks loop' towards this quarry.)

By 1926 the OS Maps marked the 'Whitehouse Lime Works and Quarry' as 'Disused' with the tramway having been lifted.

Today it is still possible to see the position of the sidings and to follow the line of the tramway from quarries to kilns (though as much of this is on private land it is necessary to seek prior permission from the landowner). The still-impressive kilns now have listed building status. A signposted public footpath, initially following the track leading from the crossroads on the B6342 road towards Ritton White House, can be used to cross the land below the Ewesley and Ritton White House quarries. Although this 'footpath' is of road proportions, cars may not be driven along it as it is clearly marked as being private property. (It is necessary for cars to be parked at the side of the B6342 road.) There are good views from this hillside footpath towards the kilns, the former Rothbury branch railway, the Fontburn viaduct and the Fontburn reservoir beyond. Alternatively it is possible to view much of the alignment of the tramway (on its embankment) from various parts of the road linking the B6342 with Fontburn reservoir, and from the top of the reservoir dam. Note that the wider sections of the reservoir approach road are passing places and not car parks!

Chapter Nine

The Proposed Alnwick & Rothbury Railway of 1890

Two documents have recently come to light regarding a proposed railway, privately promoted, from Alnwick to Rothbury which would have served several limestone quarries and works in the area, and might, if constructed, have extended their period of use. The heading for the first document is reproduced below:

ALNWICK & CANONGATE LOCAL BOARD OF HEALTH.

PROPOSED RAILWAY BETWEEN ALNWICK AND ROTHBURY.

REPORT OF SPECIAL COMMITTEE.

To THE CHAIRMAN AND MEMBERS OF THE LOCAL BOARD OF HEALTH. Alnwick, 3rd June, 1890.

It consisted of a report of a special committee which had met on 5th February, 1890 reporting that the members had collected '...all the information they could...' relating to the proposed extension to the local railway system.

Various attempts had been made between the 1840s to the 1880s to extend the rural north Northumberland railway network. These had included:

- the Northumberland Central Railway from Morpeth to Wooler and Kelso, passing between Alnwick and Rothbury across Rimside Moor,
- a branch line from Acklington, south of Alnwick, to Rothbury, and
- an extension of the Rothbury branch to Thropton, Alnham and Hedgeley, thence towards Wooler.

None of these proposed lines, described in other published works, was constructed, for the reasons of lack of finance and other support.

By 1890 the railways in the area consisted of three routes. The first was the branch from Bilton (soon to be named Alnmouth) to Alnwick, which had opened in 1850. This was operated by the North Eastern Railway. The same company had opened the line from Alnwick to Cornhill and Coldstream via Whittingham, in 1887, with trains on both of these lines using a new, improved, station at Alnwick. To the west the North British Railway's branch line from Scots Gap to Rothbury had opened in 1870.

Some 11 miles of sparsely-populated and sharply-undulating countryside lay between Alnwick and Rothbury, though the area did include several mines and quarries. The report recognised this and concluded with the following:

> **Your Committee are well aware that to make a line remunerative it is necessary that not only there should be local traffic but that a connection should be formed with a general system, so as to lead to through communication, and are strongly of opinion that both these essentials would be secured by the line now proposed, and therefore would recommend that the Board authorize the Committee to place the necessary information before the owners of property interested in the scheme and the directors of the railway company.**
>
> **Signed,**
> **CHAS. PERCY, Chairman.**
> **JOHN JAS. HORSLEY.**
> **RICHD. ARCHBOLD.**
> **JAMES HEATLEY, Hon. Sec.**
> **GEOFFREY WILSON, Surveyor.**

The report included quotations from letters and documents, dating from the 1860s, relating to the proposed Northumberland Central Railway. The Duke of Northumberland had failed to support this line on the grounds that it would not serve Alnwick. An alternative route had then been suggested which would have diverted the line from Pauperhaugh, near to the site of the Brinkburn Ironworks, via Longframlington and Greensfield to Alnwick. This proposal, like the original, did not come to fruition. The 1890 proposal was to differ in some details in that the line was proposed to start at Rothbury, cross the River Coquet by means of a sandstone bridge or viaduct (of 92 ft in height according to a local resident), then to pass to the south of Longframlington and approach Alnwick via Newton-on-the-Moor.

One of the reasons for the chosen route was the existence of several limestone quarries and limeworks to the south of Alnwick.

> *Old Quarries to south of Whittle.*—Both lime and coal have been worked here, and could be so again if there were railway facilities.
>
> *Limestone Quarries and Works at Newton-on-the-Moor.*—These are to the south-east of the village. Wm J. Gowan is owner and manager of quarry and limekiln. It is mountain limestone, 30ft. thick in strata. The quarry is dry and the stone easy to get, any amount of it available. The lime is used on farms, and in the town of Alnwick at present; also for road metal in the neighbourhood. There is also 7-yard and 8-yard limestone in the coalpit.
>
> A *Chalybeate Spring* is to the west of Newton village, on the property of Major Widdrington. This village being situated on the top of a hill might become a small health resort for invalids and visitors were there a railway near it.
>
> There is a *Limestone Quarry* and *old kiln* belonging to Major Widdrington to the west of turnpike road, formerly worked, and could be re-opened again.
>
> *Old Limestone Quarries*, westward of Newton-on-the-Moor, workable still. Owned by Mr Riddell, of Felton Park.

Other potential sources of mineral traffic which were quoted in evidence included the collieries at Newton-on-the-Moor and at Shilbottle, also the Fanny Pit at Framlington [*sic*]. Remarkably the report also referred to the proximity of the Brinkburn Ironworks with its colliery and 'tram line' which had closed some 30 years previously!

> **BRINKBURN IRONWORKS AND COLLIERY.**
>
> The iron stone was got in a pit in boulders—splendid for mixing with Cleveland iron. Coal is to be got in the pit also, and it was used for smelting the ironstone when the works were going. Bad to work at present from quantity of redd and expenses of cartage. It used to be 7s a ton to Acklington Station, and 4s 6d a ton to Brinkburn Station, of the N.B.Ry. Formerly worked in the pit or mine by a shaft and run down to works by a tram line. Whinstone, sandstone, limestone, fire-clays, coal and ironstone all to be got in quantities here.

(The use of this mid-19th century 'tram line', to supply the works at Brinkburn, was described in an earlier volume in this series.)

The second document was written by a local resident, Mr J. Anderson of Long Framlington [*sic*]. He wrote in support of the railway project referring to a 'host of minerals' being available in the area. This letter appears to have been sent to one of the signatories named above, namely Richard Archbold, though the spelling and grammar throughout make parts difficult to read (*see overleaf*).

Mr Anderson included, as an appendix, a list of the minerals which were to be found in the area near to the route of the proposed railway, though the letter does not make it clear as to how many locations the list refers:

Sir, I will give you the minerals that I know a long side of the Railway if it come' [*sic*].

Whinstone	
Limestone	30 feet
Read [Red?] Fire Clay	60 feet
Coal	
Fire Clay	5 feet
Freestone	92 feet
Iron Stone Shale	30 feet
Limestone	18 feet
Fire Clay	8 feet
House Coal	
Iron Stone Shale	20 feet
Fire Clay	6 feet

The most of the pople about hear think it will come {*sic*].

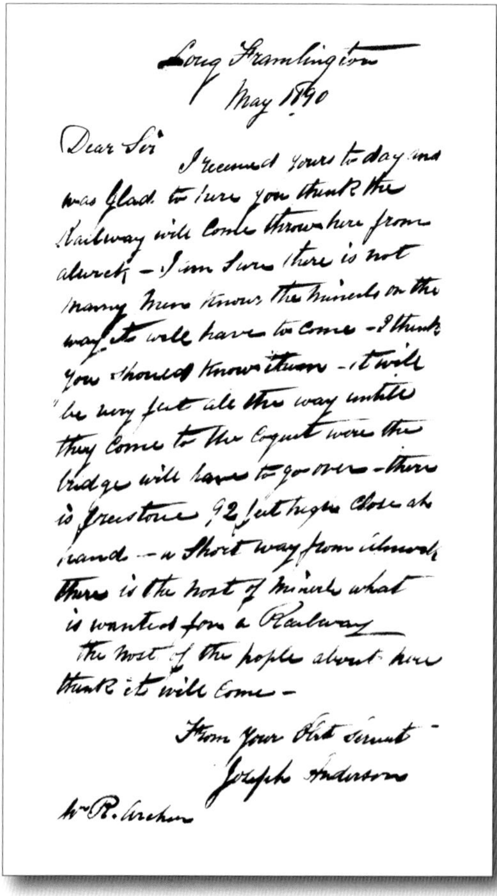

Long Framlington
1 May 1890

Dear Sir
I received yours to day and was glad to here you think the Railway will come throw here from alnwick – I am sure there is not many men knows the minerals on the way it will have to come – I think you should know them – it will be very flat all the way untill they come to the Coquet were the bridge will have to go over – there is freestone 92 feet high close at hand – a short way from alnwick there is the most of minerls what is wanted for a Railway
the most of the pople about here think it will come –

From your Obt servnt
Joseph Anderson

Mr R. Archer

This optimism, expressed in the last sentence of Mr Anderson's letter referring to the railway proposal, was not to be realized. It is believed that the lack of support from the Duke of Northumberland ultimately led to its failure. Instead, the local lime quarries and works were soon to close. The coal from Longframlington's new colliery was, in the future, to be transported by an overhead cableway to Whittle, whilst both Shilbottle and Whittle collieries were to obtain new outlets for their coal, via rail links to the main Newcastle to Berwick line. Unsurprisingly, there was to be no revival for Brinkburn Ironworks either.

Chapter Ten

Other Limestone Railways?

In addition to those already described, there were various other limestone quarries in the Alnwick and Berwick districts and some of these were quite extensive, possessing large kilns. Unfortunately documentary evidence relating to many of these quarries is conspicuous by its absence. In addition local newspaper coverage of their activities is exceedingly sparse. However, on-the-ground inspections of some of the sites, and the study of old maps, have suggested that other tramway systems may have existed.

18 - Botany Quarry and Limekilns

One such site is the Botany Quarry and lime kilns at Tillside in the parish of Chillingham. The site is clearly marked on the first edition Ordnance Survey maps. Two kilns are known to have been operated at this site on the edge of Hepburn Moor, both served by the adjacent quarry. OS maps surveyed at the end of the 19th century mark the quarry as 'Disused' and it is likely that limeburning finished here at some date in the second half of that century. The quarry lies on the south side of the hill road leading from the A1 road at North Charlton towards Hepburn and Chillingham. Various small coal pits near to this road may have been the source of coal for the kilns. A well, situated near to the south-east corner of the quarry, may have provided the water for converting the freshly roasted quicklime into slaked lime, the latter being safer to transport and use. The slightly wider quarry floor at this point could have been the site of a slaking floor.

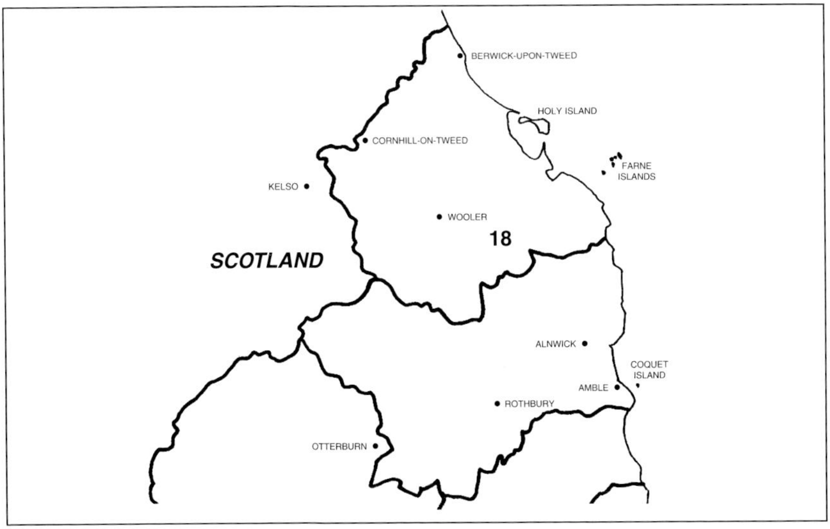

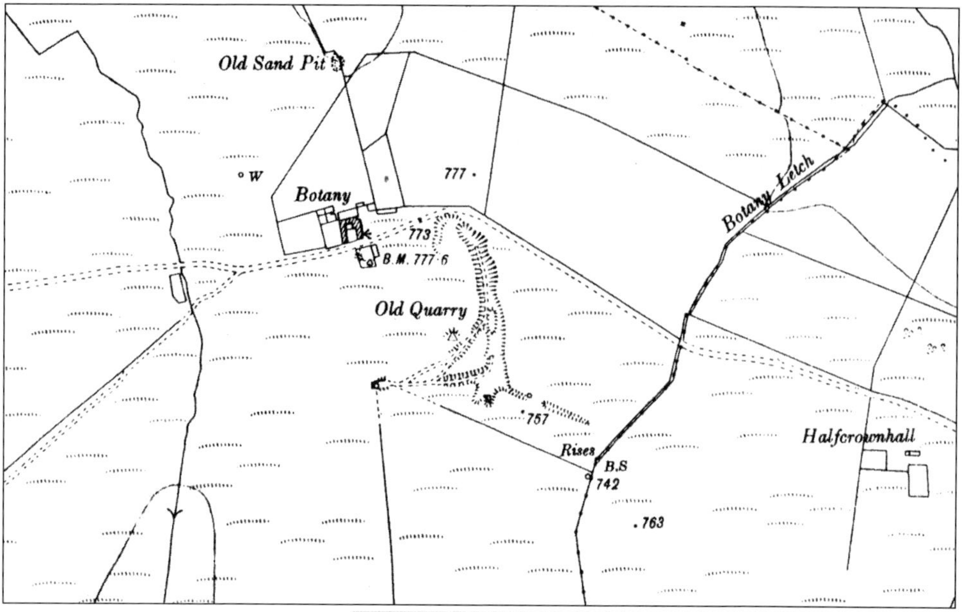

Above: This early Ordnance Survey map shows the position of Botany Quarry to the south side of the unfenced road which links North Charlton to the east with Hepburn to the west.

Ordnance Survey, Crown copyright, All Rights Reserved

Right: This view shows part of the limestone face towards the north end of Botany Quarry. Over 100 years of erosion have caused parts of the face to collapse but the quality of the stone can be clearly seen.

Author

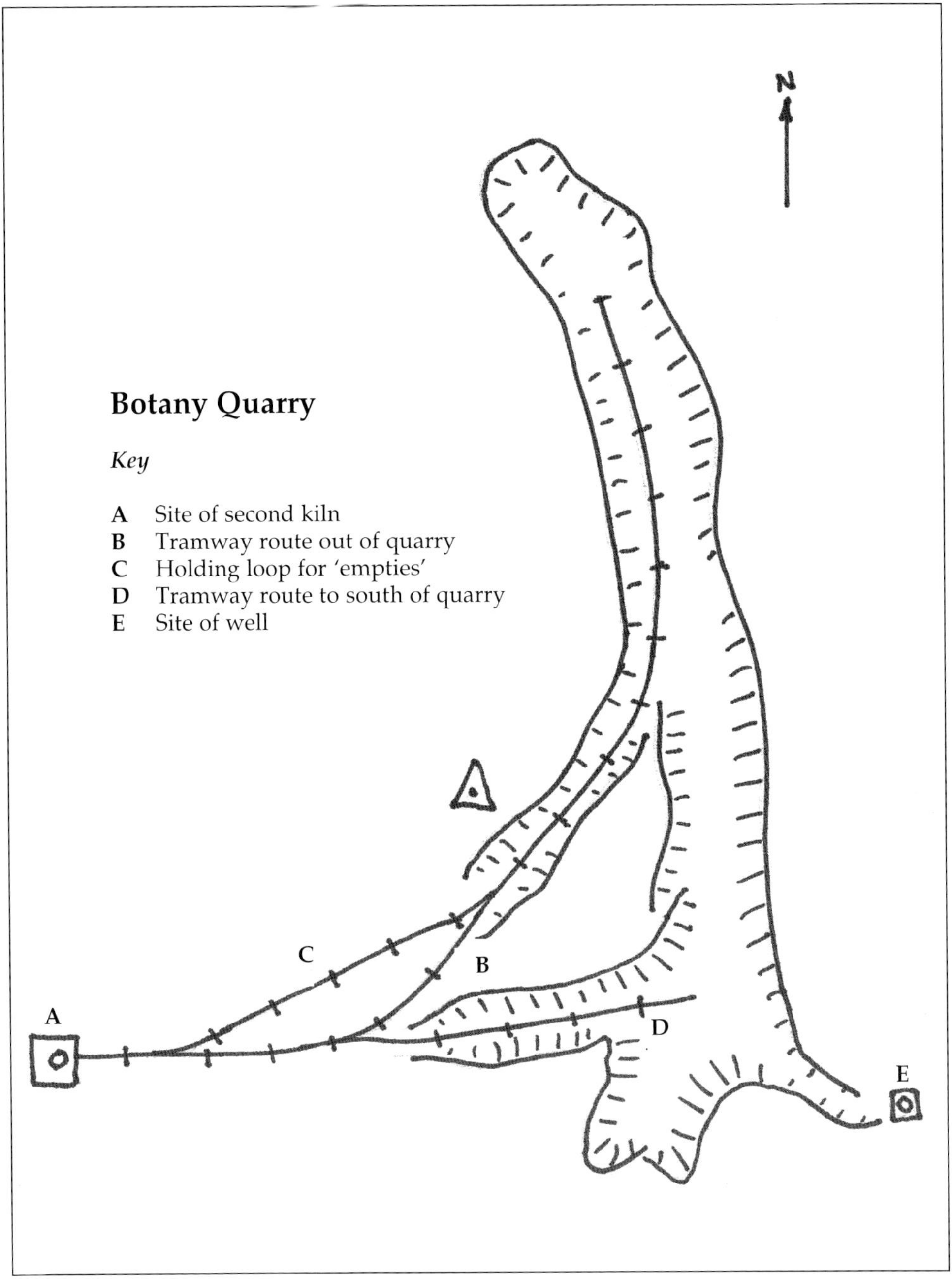

This plan of Botany Quarry suggests the possible routes of a tramway serving the kilns and their individual roles. It is based on on-the-ground study as well as cartographic evidence. *Author*

This view shows the curving route leading out of the north part of the quarry. The gradient is gentle and even, thus facilitating the movement of stone towards the kiln. *Author*

The younger of the two Botany Quarry kilns is the only one to survive. This view is taken from its south western side. The grazing of livestock in the field has caused some erosion around the top of the kiln. *Author*

One of the kilns, the older of the two, lies immediately to the west of the quarry close to where the 'trackway' leads from the stone faces. The first edition OS map (surveyed 1860-1) indicates what might be interpreted as the remains of a small tramway leading to the kiln top. By this date the second kiln was the kiln being used for roasting the lime. (A 'trig point' now occupies the kiln mound in this elevated position.)

The newer of the two kilns was also located to the west of the quarry but approximately south-west of the first kiln. Further study of the first edition OS map indicates a 'trackway' leading towards the second kiln from the southern end of the quarry. However, the 'trackway' from the north end is more interesting in that it splits to form two alternative routes, forming a loop or 'passing place' on leaving the quarry. The more southerly of these alternative routes curves from the quarry floor, then straightens, before joining the route from the south end of the quarry and leading towards the kiln top. The other, more northerly alternative, appears to form a 'short cut'.

A site inspection in 2010, using a copy of the map as a guide, showed that the gradient on the first of the alternative tracks is very even and that the curve is both gentle and almost regular. The 'short cut' alternative is very different. At the kiln end, the alignment is almost level; however it becomes much steeper as it enters the quarry and descends to join the first route.

It is tempting to suggest that the route with the even gradient could have been the route along which stone was hauled from the northern end of the quarry. If a small line of rails had existed this would have facilitated the work of horses, with the gentle curve producing little friction between the rails and the wheel flanges of the hauled vehicles. The level section of the 'short cut' could, conceivably, have been a storage line for empty wagons waiting return to the quarry face. The steep gradient of the lower part of the line would have permitted their return to the quarry face by gravity when an initial 'shove' from a quarryman had set them in motion. A system using ordinary carts and horses would not have needed such an arrangement.

It must be emphasized that this is speculation for there has been no discovery of old rails in the vicinity, either *in situ* or in use as fence posts or suchlike. Furthermore no documentary evidence has come to light to describe the quarry workings. However, the ground surface at this site is very 'sticky' after prolonged rain, and the existence of small lines of rails would have made the lifting of the limestone from the quarry very much easier.

In an earlier volume it was suggested that brickworks, other than those where a small railway has been confirmed, may have employed small lines of rails for facilitating the movement of clay, or transport of bricks and tiles. It is quite likely that the same line of thought could be applied to some of the local lime quarries and limeworks, especially where these were extensive. The large quarries at Oxford, south of Berwick, may come into this category, though it must be emphasized, once again, that no cartographic or other documentary evidence has presented itself regarding the use of rail lines to either of the kilns at this site. Flooding of some lower quarry levels, agricultural activities, erosion, some tipping and the development of gravelled roads has probably eliminated any on-the-ground evidence.

As described in Volume One of this series of books, Colonel Leather organized his forestry plantations and railway as a 'model' for others to copy. For this he was awarded medals by the Royal English Arboricultural Society (later the Royal Forestry Society), two of which are shown here. *Leather Family Archive courtesy of Michael Greene*

Trains on the Heatherslaw Railway always run with the locomotive boiler leading. To achieve this it is necessary to turn locomotives at the end of each run. This is the new palisaded turntable at the Etal end of the line with the table set for the platform road. *Author*

Chapter Eleven

A Picture Gallery

In 1981 my first railway book was published. It told the history of a line which transported stone in the Wirral peninsula. For some years I had tried to obtain extra photographs to illustrate this modest volume. Harry Paar, the well-known railway historian said to me: 'Roger, you can end up waiting forever for photographs to appear. Go ahead and publish your book and don't be surprised if you receive many offers of photographs afterwards!' I followed Harry's advice.

However, to my huge embarrassment, the first two pictures to arrive after publication were pictures illustrating the use, for a very brief period, of a steam locomotive on the line, which I had described as having always relied upon gravity and horse haulage! Fortunately the *Railway Magazine* published an article for me just two years later in which I could update and correct the story.

I have, therefore, not been surprised to receive several contacts from persons who have provided some additional details and pictures to update the stories of the lines described in Volumes One to Three of this series, some even identifying themselves or family relatives in the pictures. Unfortunately there has been insufficient time to conduct the further research necessary to corroborate some of this extra information.

I have been told of three 'new' lines to incorporate into the list of minor railways. The first was associated with a stone quarry on Branxton Moor, between Wooler and Cornhill, in the far north-west of the Berwick District. Cartographic evidence shows that the quarry was in use between about 1918 and World War II. Railway remains were extant in the quarry when the present farmer took over Branxton Moor Farm. The second line was yet another 'target railway' operated by the Ministry of Defence, on this occasion in Upper Coquetdale in the Cheviot Hills. It was located to the east of the River Coquet just to the south of Barrowburn Farm at Windyhaugh, not far from Alwinton. It was used in World War II, and the targets were hauled by means of a system of cables. The third was a line, laid at the side of the River Till at Twizell, by contractors extracting stones from the river for making concrete for the building of the nearby railway viaduct.

Various 'new' photographs have become available since the publication of the first three books in this series. Some of these relate to lines in this volume and have been incorporated at the relevant places. Others illustrate lines already described in the first three volumes and the opportunity has been taken to reproduce them here as a short 'Gallery' rather than wait, perhaps for a long time, before they could be incorporated into reprints or new editions. Notable amongst these are several photographs, taken in the early years of the 20th century, of Long Dyke colliery at Shilbottle. In addition there is a collection of photographs taken soon after W.T. Bathgate closed his quarry at Ward's Hill in the 1960s, but showing the plant and remains of the rails and a locomotive. Others provide additional views of steam in action at Amble and different views of the locomotives at, for example, Heatherslaw and Longhoughton Quarry, near Alnwick. Some add to the 'social history', associated with the lines.

Locomotive *Bunty* (Alan Keef 85R/2010) works hard as it ascends the steep gradient into Etal station with a heavy train in the autumn of 2011. The railway, hidden behind the trees on the right, runs parallel to the River Till along its entire route from Heatherslaw Mill to Etal.

Author

The locomotive *Richborough* will be one of the first two steam locomotives to be operated by the Aln Valley Railway. It is owned by the line's Mechanical Engineer Michael Fairnington. This photograph was taken when steam was raised for the first time after a full refurbishment. *Inset:* This is the works plate newly refitted to *Richborough*. At the time of writing (April 2012) the locomotive is on loan to, and operating at, the Bo'ness & Kinneil Railway in Scotland but will eventually be based at the Aln Valley Railway's base at Alnwick (Lionheart). *(Both) Author*

Careful inspection of the route of the route of the second Shilbottle to Alnwick waggonway, especially where it passes through woodland and crosses the Cawledge Burn, reveals a variety of posts, pieces of rail and pieces of metal which evaded the attentions of the scrapman when the line was lifted. *D.P. Dalby Collection*

This photograph of the colliery at Long Dyke, Shilbottle was clearly taken on a 'working day' with steam from the engines prominent. In the background is the village of Bilton Banks which was, with the exception of one building, razed to the ground after the closure of the colliery, the occupants having to move elsewhere. *Author's Collection*

The one building that survived the demolition of Bilton Banks village was the former Manager's house which survives as a private house alongside the Shilbottle to Alnmouth road just a few yards away from the gateway to the track which formerly led into the colliery. *Author*

Several photographs have come to light illustrating Long Dyke Colliery at Shilbottle at the start of the 20th century. This print is marked 'Shilbottle Colliery ready for bettering'. Clearly several improvements were planned. *David 'Hector' Brewis Collection via Ken Middlemist*

This photograph, taken around the same time as the previous one, shows the 'old screens' with small, wooden-sided loaded coal tubs being propelled up the slope by hand for grading into lumps of various sizes. *David 'Hector' Brewis Collection via Ken Middlemist*

In the centre men are loading 'smalls' into wooden tubs whilst nearby some refurbishment or repairs to metal-sided tubs is taking place. The original photograph is marked as being taken in 1904 by a photographer with the surname of 'Dunn'.

David 'Hector' Brewis Collection via Ken Middlemist

This 1904 picture was taken at the time when Long Dyke Colliery was being refurbished. Here a group of men, using a type of sheerlegs crane, are creating the foundations for a new winding engine for the pit. *David 'Hector' Brewis Collection via Ken Middlemist*

This delightful picture shows local carter W. Wood with his horse and cart with which he will be collecting some landsale coal for local delivery. The photograph is captioned 'bait time', the local term for a lunch break. *David 'Hector' Brewis Collection via Ken Middlemist*

After Long Dyke Colliery closed a new Shilbottle Colliery was opened on the south-east side of Shilbottle village. This aerial photograph was taken towards the end of the life of this pit. Many of the buildings were subsequently demolished but some, including the former smithy, survive as a private house and farm shop. *Geoff Waters Collection via Ken Middlemist*

No. 45, one of Shilbottle Colliery's 'Austerity' saddle tanks (RSH 7113 built in 1943) was photographed propelling an empty hopper wagon at the landsale yard sidings, adjacent to the level crossing with the Shilbottle to Warkworth road. This locomotive worked at Shilbottle in 1968 and 1969, being broken up for scrap in March 1973. *Gordon Hall*

The engine shed at Shilbottle, depicted here, was of the two-road variety. Locomotive No. 45, having completed its shift has just had its saddle tank replenished with water. *Gordon Hall*

Whittle Colliery's first locomotive was the Peckett-built 0-4-0 saddle tank named *Bella* (Works No. 1628) built in 1924. By the time that this picture was taken in November 1966 it was bereft of its nameplates and stored. It was finally scrapped in March 1968. *Ken Page*

Ivy (HL3749/1921) was Whittle Colliery's second locomotive and is shown here stored in the 'Heap Road' on 8th November, 1966 just two months before it was converted into scrap metal. By this time it had lost its name and its works plate has been removed. *Ken Page*

This painting, dated 1822, shows a horse-drawn waggon of coal approaching Spittal via the waggonway which was formerly used for transporting stone for the construction of the Spittal jetty. A 1930 map (by Priestley) shows the 'top end' of the line as originating at collieries on Spring Hill. The location shown is Spittal beach. *Berwick Museum*

The author recently purchase this picture postcard via the internet. It depicts the jetty at Spittal close to the mouth of the River Tweed. By the date of this photograph, taken in the latter half of the 19th century, coal from the Scremerston collieries was being taken away over North Eastern Railway metals and was not arriving at Spittal via the former waggonway. *Author's Collection*

The shipping of coal from Amble had ceased by 1970 and the last of the steam locomotives, which had transported the final coal from Hauxley Colliery, were either scrapped or moved elsewhere. Locomotive No. 28 hauls a long train of empty hoppers back to Hauxley Colliery in the last year of its life. *Ken Page*

The yard of Longhoughton station, on the East Coast main line, is one of the sites where the Aln Valley Railway stores and prepares stock and track panels ready to move to the new Alnwick (Lionheart) station (its construction had started at the time of writing). This view shows the main line with the yard being behind the buildings on the right. *Author's Collection*

Two additional 1968 photographs have come to light showing the Hudson Hunslet diesel locomotives at Longhoughton Quarry shortly after the rails in the quarry had been lifted. The locomotive with 'No 1' chalked on its cab was works number 1947 whilst the other was works number 1992. Both were scrapped by September 1969. *(Both) Dr C.G. Down*

The drift mines at Ward's Hill were operated by W.T. Bathgate from the late 1940s until the early 1960s and produced crushed coal for his lime works at Greenleighton. Both of these pictures were taken in August 1967 after the mines had closed. The upper picture shows a former trackbed leading to one of the mines whilst the lower picture shows part of the plant with an elevator leading up to the crusher. *(Both) Dr C.G. Down*

Bathgate moved two of his Ruston locomotives to Ward's Hill Quarry from Greenleighton. One returned to Greenleighton but the other was cannibalized. The engine was used to power a portable screen where the crushed stone was graded and this is shown in the upper picture inside a corrugated iron shed. After the engine was removed the remainder of the locomotive, including the frames, gearbox and wheels, was dumped at the side of the incline leading up from the quarry as seen in the lower picture. *(Both) Dr C.G. Down*

This August 1968 photograph was taken with the camera pointing up the gradient from the quarry towards the plant near the summit of Ward's Hill. In the foreground are the remains of Ruston 235653 whilst the plant buildings and water tower form part of the background. The remains of the Ruston were scrapped around 1969. *Dr C.G. Down*

This 1968 photograph shows Bathgate's quarry at Ward's Hill after stone extraction had ceased. Lengths of rail abound, some torn up, some still *in situ*. The frames and bodies of various side-tipper wagons litter the gradient leading to the quarry floor. The steep cable-worked incline up to the plant is on the right of the picture. *Dr C.G. Down*

No views of the narrow gauge locomotive MR8614/1941 have been discovered whilst it was working at Ewesley Quarry. However, it was later sold to Ramshaw Fluorspar Mine in County Durham, where it was photographed in the gloom of the locomotive shed. *Dr C.G. Down*

Acknowledgements

I would like to acknowledge with much gratitude the assistance provided by the following 'official' organizations, individuals and companies that have been very patient and generous in responding to requests for assistance with my research:

Northumberland Record Office at Woodhorn, (formerly at Gosforth and Morpeth), Berwick-on-Tweed Record Office (Linda Bankier and Carole Pringle), Durham Record Office, Tyne and Wear Archives Service, Somerset Record Office, Powys County Archives, Northumberland County Libraries at Berwick-upon-Tweed, Morpeth and Alnwick, City of Dundee Library, British Library (Map Library and Newspaper Library), the National Archive at Kew, the Parliamentary Archive, Dundee City Archive, Tweeddale Press Group (*Berwick Advertiser*), *Northumberland Gazette*, *The Times*, Lloyds Register of Shipping, Berwick-upon-Tweed Civic Society, Berwick-upon-Tweed Preservation Trust (John Smithson), Ordnance Survey, Durham Mining Museum, Industrial Railway Society (Dave Holroyde), Industrial Locomotive Society (Russell Wear and Allan C. Baker), the Historical Model Railway Society (Peter Swift), North of England Open Air Museum at Beamish, National Railway Museum Library, Companies House, Narrow Gauge Railway Society (Clive Walters), the Ruston Archive (Ray Hooley), Devon Railway Centre, Fife Family History Society, Scottish Stone Liaison Group, Smiths Gore (James Boulton), Plateway Press, Forestry Commission (Kielder District), Australian War Memorial Research Centre, National Railway Museum (C.P. Atkins), Department of Veterans Affairs in Canberra, Australia (Richard Reid), Royal Artillery Museum (Matthew Buck and Paul Evans), Berwick-on-Tweed Museum, Wooler Information Centre, Glendale Gateway Trust, Northumberland County Council Conservation Team, Alan Keef Ltd, Northumberland National Park Authority, Northumbrian Water, Newcastle Local Studies Centre, Defence Estates, Ministry of Defence (Chris Livsey), Public Monument and Sculpture Association, Directorate of History and Heritage of the Canadian Department of National Defence, National Library of Canada and National Archives of Canada, Northumbria Rail, Aln Valley Railway Society (Vera Mallon, Gavin Head, Ken Middlemist and William Stafford), Road Roller Association, Geological Society of London, British Geological Survey, Building Research Establishment, the Lagan Group, TARMAC Ltd, Hanson UK (David Weeks), Stirling Stone Group, LH Group Services (Henry Noon), Howick Estates, Northumberland Estates, Wallington Estates, Joicey Estates, Lilburn Estates Farming Partnership, Chillingham Castle (Sir Humphrey Wakefield), UAP, George F. White (Land Agents), Bailiffgate Museum in Alnwick (Gemma Taylor), the Thorneycroft Register (Alan Sleight), Whitstable Museum (Craig Bowen), Railsearch Images (Thomas Carrick), the Irving Gallery, the Road Locomotive Society, the Royal Forestry Society, the National Trust (Harry Beamish), Leather Family Archives (Michael Greene), Belford Local History Society (Fiona Renner-Thompson), Taylor Wimpey, Bamburgh Golf Club (the late Gordon McKeag), Glasgow University Archive Services, Derbyshire Local Studies Library, and the Mitchell Library in Glasgow.

I have made use of the website of the Durham Mining Museum, the 'keystothepast' website of the Northumberland and Durham County Councils, and the 'Northumberland Communities' website of the Northumberland Archive Service. The website 'Access to Archives' (a2a) has been invaluable in enabling me to identify and locate a huge variety of documents. The internet, generally, has been a valuable research tool allowing me to access records, for example in Canada and Australia, which I would not otherwise have discovered. I have used census records available both on CD-ROM and on-line.

The records of the Industrial Railway Society, the Industrial Locomotive Society and the Narrow Gauge Railway Society have been invaluable in providing me with details of the various locomotives mentioned in the text. In return I have been pleased to pass on to them details which have not previously been in their records, or corrections arising out of my research. In particular I offer my grateful thanks to Dave Holroyde of the IRS and NGRS who kindly read through the manuscript, offered much helpful advice and corrected locomotive and other details.

In a recently published book on railways, an author apologized for not including the names of all of the '101 private individuals' who had provided assistance with his book. I would like to offer my grateful thanks to the 202 individuals (at least!) who have found the time to provide help during my eight years of research for this book. (Your assistance, your letters, your emails and your telephone calls have been very much appreciated!) Those who have offered photographs for the book will see their name appearing beneath those that have been used. If a photograph has not been used it may well have provided very useful information which I have incorporated into the book. If you have provided me with information, or directed me towards sources of information, I'm sure you will be pleased to recognise the relevant material in the text!

However, it is likely that there will be some errors or omissions. For these I accept full responsibility. I would be delighted to receive any photographs, corrections or additions which would make the descriptions of these minor railways more complete!

Every attempt has been made to identify the copyright owners of the illustrations used. However, some were obtained from unmarked photographic prints or old picture postcards purchased, for example, at postcard fairs. Often these have no means of identification and have thus been described as being from the 'author's collection'. My sincere apologies if your print has been used without permission.

Abbreviations for Locomotive Builders

AK	Alan Keef Ltd, Ross-on-Wye
HE	Hunslet Engine Co. Ltd, Leeds
HL	R. & W. Hawthorn, Leslie & Co. Ltd, Newcastle-upon-Tyne
MR	Motor Rail Ltd, Simplex Works, Bedford
MW	Manning, Wardle & Co. Ltd, Boyne Works, Hunslet, Leeds
P	Peckett & Sons Ltd, St George, Bristol
RH	Ruston & Hornsby Ltd, Lincoln
RSH	Robert Stephenson and Hawthorns Ltd

Bibliography

The following books and journals, in whole or in part, contain further reading or photographs related to some of the minor railways and industries in Northern Northumberland; all of these have been consulted.

The North British Railway in Northumberland by G.W.M. Sewell: Merlin Books
Main Line Railways of Northumberland by C.R. Warn: Frank Graham
Waggonways and Early Railways of Northumberland by C.R. Warn: Frank Graham
Rural Branch Lines of Northumberland by C.R. Warn: Frank Graham
Railways of the Northumberland Coalfield by C.R. Warn: Frank Graham
Industrial Railways in Northumberland and County Durham in the Days of Steam by Malcolm Castledine: Book Law Publications
A Regional History of the Railways of Great Britain: Volume IV The North East by Ken Hoole: David & Charles
Railway Stations of the North East by Ken Hoole: David & Charles
Forgotten Railways, North East England by Ken Hoole: David & Charles
Lindisfarne's Limestone Past by Roger C. Jermy: Northumberland Libraries
Lindisfarne Holy Island by Deidre O'Sullivan and Robert Young: English Heritage
Railways in Northumberland by Alan Young: Martin Bairstow Publishing
The Alnwick to Cornhill Railway 1887 to 1953 by Mary H. Brown: The Aln and Breamish Local History Society
The Alnwick and Cornhill Railway by John Addyman and John Mallon: North Eastern Railway Association
Industrial Locomotives of Northumberland: compiled by L.G. Charlton and Colin E. Mountford: Industrial Railway Society (a new edition, compiled and edited by Dave Holroyde, is in preparation)
Lost Railways of Northumberland by Robert Kinghorn: Countryside Books
Industrial Archaeology of North-East England (Volumes 1 & 2) by Frank Atkinson: David & Charles
Dam Builders' Railways from Durham's Dales to the Border by H.D. Bowtell: Plateway Press
The North Sunderland Railway by A. Wright: Oakwood Press
The Rothbury Branch by S.C. Jenkins: Oakwood Press
The Amble Branch by Bartle Rippon: Kestrel Railway Books
The Alnwick Branch by Bartle Rippon: Kestrel Railway Books
Border Country Branch Line Album by Neil Caplan: Ian Allan
Middleton, The Leathers and the Colonel's Railway by Tony Lee: Belford Local History Society
Memories of the LNER in Rural Northumberland by Allan Stobbs: published by the author
The Collieries of Northumberland Vol. 1 by James Tuck: Trade Union Printing Services
Longframlington: A look at the village through photos and stories by John West: published by the author
Wooler to Hexham and Return by Ken Veitch: The John Sinclair Railway Museum, Killingworth
Views of Wooler and Glendale by Derek Fairnington and Roger Mikel: MacLean Press, Wooler
Reflections, The Breamish Valley and Ingram by Sarah Wilson: Northern Heritage
We Can Mind The Time; Memories of Craster People: Ed. Colin Biott: Craster Community Development Trust
A History of Northumberland and Newcastle Upon Tyne by Leslie W. Hepple: Phillimore & Co.
Colliery Engineering: November 1930 Edition
Railway Bylines: various editions: Irwell Press
A Short History of Embleton Whinston Quarry; D. Malthouse; privately published monograph

Various newspapers have been consulted including copies of the *Berwick Advertiser*, the *Northumberland Gazette* and the *Cumberland News*, also trade journals including the *Stone Trade Journal, Contract Journal* and *Machinery Market*.

Bound volumes of the *Berwick Advertiser* are located in the offices of the company which still produces this newspaper in Berwick, though it is probably easier to conduct inspections at Berwick Public Library or at Berwick Record Office where most editions of this newspaper (and others covering the local area) are available on microfilm. It is advisable to book ahead to reserve a microfilm reader at both places.

Bound volumes of the *Northumberland Gazette* (and other early local newspapers which covered the Alnwick area) are held at the Bailiffgate Museum in Alnwick although they are not currently available for inspection. A few bound volumes, free to view, are kept at Alnwick Public Library. Other editions have been microfilmed and are available for inspection at the same library.

Microfilm copies of Berwick, Alnwick, Carlisle, Gateshead and Newcastle newspapers, also other journals, can be viewed at the Newspaper Library in Colindale, London, though it is essential to make reservations in advance.

The many original documents consulted can be found at various locations, including the Berwick-on-Tweed Record Office, the Northumberland Record Office at Woodhorn (formerly at Gosforth and Morpeth), the Durham University Archive, the National Archives at Kew, and in other public and private collections (see 'Acknowledgements'). Many of the colliery records, formerly with the Northumberland Record Office, have been moved recently to the North of England Institute of Mining and Mechanical Engineers in Westgate Road, Newcastle-upon-Tyne.

I was very fortunate in that various people contacted me, during the preparation of this series of books, offering photographs, maps and other illustrative material. I was offered this picture postcard, regarding 'Drusilla's, Berwick'. I was not aware of any location near Berwick-upon-Tweed with this name, operating a narrow gauge railway, and in any case, the style of the buildings depicted did not seem to fit with the architecture of the Berwick District. Drusilla's is actually a Zoo Park located at Berwick, near Eastbourne, on the south coast of England! Its 2 ft gauge railway has, for some years, been operated by small diesel-mechanical locomotives. Other researchers beware! *Author's Collection*